This is a wonderful book to help Christians recognize and utilize the provisions that our Lord has made for our spiritual health and growth. Too often believers are tempted to look for big, unusual events or experiences for spiritual strength and encouragement while neglecting the regular, comparatively unimpressive provisions like Scripture, baptism, the Lord's Supper, and prayer. Yet it is precisely these latter, "ordinary" provisions that the Lord Jesus has given to utilize to build us up in faith and establish us in His grace. Just as physical health is better pursued by commitment to careful nutrition rather than remedial medical intervention, so the pathway to spiritual health is dependent on the ordinary means of grace and not occasional, extraordinary experiences. J. Ryan Davidson understands that and wants God's people to understand it as well. He clearly explains what the Bible teaches about the importance of the ordinary means that Christ has provided for His church. This book is pastorally wise, confessionally faithful, and spiritually helpful. I highly recommend it.

Tom Ascol
Pastor, Grace Baptist Church in Cape Coral, Florida
Executive Director, Founders Ministries
****

This little book addresses what we might call the "core business of the Church of Christ on earth," the ordinary means of grace. The fact that that last expression will be lost on many readers today is illustrative of where we have ended up as the Church of God. The "means" addressed here refer to the "bread and butter" of Christian discipleship — the provision of God for Christian growth and health and for the Christians' regular awareness of the living presence of the Lord around, beside, and within them. The

Word and Sacraments are the very means by which our triune God communicates Himself to His people. This book will help people from various traditions in learning to appreciate and benefit from this awesome divine provision.

Liam Goligher
Senior Minister, Tenth Presbyterian Church
Philadelphia, PA
****

The proverbial "good things come in small packages" is an appropriate word for Ryan Davidson's *Green Pastures: A Primer on the Means of Grace*. This book will be for your soul what the diamond ring hidden inside a velvet presentation box is to a bride-to-be: pure delight. In simple, well-illustrated language, Pastor Davidson teaches us how the covenant Lord blesses His people with lavish gifts of grace. Pastors should distribute *Green Pastures* to their people, and God's people need to wonder and delight in its truths. I wish that I had read this book forty years ago!

James M. Renihan
President, IRBS Theological Seminary
Mansfield, TX
****

One of the things that binds confessional Presbyterians and Reformed Baptists together is their common commitment to a ministry shaped by the ordinary means of grace. Such a ministry is not a matter of arbitrary personal taste but driven by our understanding of exactly what God's grace is and how it becomes a reality in the lives of Christians. This short book helps in that regard, offering short, sound accounts of the Word, sacraments, and prayer in a manner that will help all of those seeking a ministry that reflects biblical priorities and teaching.

Carl R. Trueman
Professor of Biblical and Religious Studies
Grove City College
Grove City, PA
****

Green Pastures

A Primer on the Ordinary Means of Grace

****

J. Ryan Davidson

RBAP

Palmdale, CA

Requests for information should be sent to:

RBAP
349 Sunrise Terrace
Palmdale, CA 93551
rb@rbap.net
www.rbap.net

Printed in the United Kingdom by 4edge Ltd

Cover design by Marina Campagna and formatted for print by
Todd Odenath.

ISBN: 978-0-9965198-4-7

Contents

Introduction[1]

This little work is intended to discuss, in simple detail, what have been called the ordinary means of grace. For some, this phrase is unknown, and will need some explanation. Part of the reason for this book is to aid in the recovery of the biblical understanding of the particular means that the Lord has ordained for His church wherein He nurtures its faith. Our day is one of great biblical illiteracy. It is also a day, even among avid churchgoers, where substitutes have been given for the very means that the Lord has said He will use to bless His people. Sundays, in many American churches, have been turned into a time for emotionalism, entertainment, or for programmatic ministry. What have been jettisoned along the way are the simple, ordinary mechanisms that God has ordained for the growth and nourishment of His people: preaching, baptism, the Lord's Supper, and prayer. Many might even read those words and think that there must be more to church. In many corners of the West, we have taken the ministry of the church and turned it into a one-stop shop for felt needs — a

---

[1] In addition to my church family who walked with me through many of these chapters initially in a sermon series, I am indebted to my father, Tommy Davidson, for his helpful read through of this manuscript, as well as my friends, Persis Lorenti and Joey Tomlinson, for their helpful critiques. I am also grateful and blessed to have my wife Christie alongside me in the journey and am so thankful for her genuine love, helpful suggestions and edits of this manuscript. Thanks to Rich Barcellos as well for all his labors in this project.

super mall if you will, of spiritual stores. While there is nothing wrong with trying to meet the needs of others, in the process we have undervalued the very things that the Lord has commanded us to prize in our churches. With the loss of this emphasis, many Christians are under-taught, and do not even realize that the very simple ordinary means of grace are exactly what they need. Sermons have been shortened to allow for more entertainment. Baptism, in many evangelical services, has been turned into a party, focusing only on a person's decision, rather than the proclamation of God's promise. The Lord's Supper has fallen on hard times too, and in many churches is rarely practiced. Corporate prayer is kept to a minimum in order to allow for other foci. This is serious indeed, for it is through these very means that the Lord has promised to bless and grow His people.

We need a retrieval of the understanding and use of these means within our churches. Oh, would that local congregations all across this globe return to these very simple and ordinary means! Perhaps you are reading this book because you want to learn more about the "ordinary means of grace." Or maybe you are considering a different path for ministry within your own church. Perhaps you are a Baptist who is trying to understand further the Reformation roots of your own history and are seeking to learn more about how early Particular Baptists really share Reformed theology with other Protestant groups. My hope and prayer is that this little book will serve as a helpful springboard for richer and deeper study into the matter. Why would we not want the sweet communion promised in these means, and why would we not want the very voice of Christ proclaimed within them?

In a day when church growth works line the shelves of bookstores and Amazon, and in a time when many dear believers are looking for everything in their church besides the ordinary means, the call of the Scriptures is to be ever reforming according to biblical patterns of belief and worship. What an opportunity the church has always had, to assemble with the primacy placed on the ordinary channels of grace. For many pastors, the idea of numerical growth can be so tempting, and falling prey to it may mean cutting corners on the biblical commands for worship. However, the flock of the Lord needs to be fed in the pastures that He has ordained. Let us run then to His pastures...and to Him.

1

Commended to God and Means

So now, brethren, I commend you to God and to the word of His grace, which is able to build you up and give you an inheritance among all those who are sanctified. (Acts 20:32)

I have had the opportunity to travel to many parts of the world over the last decade or so to serve in various ways, often to teach pastors, seminary students, or new believers in various areas of theological training. One of the hardest things to do is to swoop in for just a few weeks, knowing that you will be leaving soon and unable to say all that could be said, and then depart knowing all the various forms of theological error with which the students will be confronted. What do you do? What do you say? And ultimately, to what do you commend them?

Toward the end of the book of Acts, some years after Christ ascended, the apostle Paul gathered with the church at Ephesus. We read of the sweet encounter the apostle had with the elders, or pastors of that church, giving them a variety of instructions. Knowing that he cannot say all there is to say, and knowing that he will likely not see them again, he says in Acts 20:28, "Therefore take heed to yourselves and to all the flock, among which the Holy Spirit has made you overseers, to shepherd the church of God which He purchased with His own blood." Later in verse 32, he says, "So now, brethren, I commend you to God and to the word of His grace, which is able to build you up and give you an inheritance among all those who are sanctified." Paul commends this people to a means of grace.

Throughout this book, we will be walking through a variety of Scripture passages that reveal to us the ordinary means of grace, the regular channels that the Lord uses to strengthen and nurture the faith of His people in the grace that Christ has wrought for them. First, however, let's examine this idea that the Lord even uses regular, or ordinary means. From this passage in Acts, I think we can see three truths regarding the reality of the ordinary means of grace. First, God builds up His people in grace. The second truth is that God uses means to grow His people in grace, and third, that God uses specified means to strengthen and increase the faith of His covenant people. Let's take these one by one and explore these realities further.

God Builds Up His People in Grace

I want to start with a quotation from the Second London [Baptist] Confession of Faith (2LCF) because I think it puts together well the doctrinal reality of our faith being strengthened, but it is also beneficial for us to undertake theology alongside the church of Christ down through the ages as we seek to understand how those who have gone before us have undertaken the study of different doctrines. Here are the words from the Confession to which I am referring:

The grace of faith, whereby the elect are enabled to

believe to the saving of their souls, is the work of the Spirit of Christ, and is ordinarily wrought by the ministry of the word. By which also, and by the administration of baptism and the Lord's Supper, prayer, and other means appointed of God, it is increased and strengthened. (2LCF 14.1)

Perhaps you have not thought about faith being a form of grace. Faith itself is a gift of grace given to believers by God. We didn't come up with faith; God grants faith and He strengthens it. He grants saving faith to all those who are redeemed and that grace through faith results in the saving of their souls. This is the work of the Spirit of Christ in their hearts. When Christ and the gospel became clear to me, it was because the Holy Spirit had first worked in my heart. It is through the ministry of the Word that faith is wrought, or birthed, in the believer (Rom. 10:14-17). But not only is saving faith a grace of God, as the Confession points out, but God also strengthens it: "By which also, and by the administration of baptism and the Lord's Supper, prayer, and other means appointed of God, it is...strengthened."

The Lord uses means both to bring about faith and to strengthen and nurture it. Let's look again at the aforementioned text. Paul, talking with these elders in his final few words to them, commends them to two things: "to God" and "to the word of his grace." Paul confidently gives these elders, and ultimately the church at Ephesus, over to God and to the word of His grace. The text tells us why — to be built up. Look at the text: "which is able to build you up and give you an inheritance among all those who are sanctified." Now this should not surprise us. Paul would say to another church, the church at Colossae, these words in Colossians 2:6-7, "As you therefore have received Christ Jesus the Lord, so walk in Him, rooted and built up in Him and established in the faith, as you have been taught, abounding in it with thanksgiving."

The God who saves us is also the God who builds us up

in Him. What Paul does is not only commend these believers to His God, but he also commends them to the means that God uses to build them up in their faith. He says, "I commend you to God and to the word of his grace, which is able to build you up." Now of course we know that the triune God is the One who builds up His people; however, in this text, it is almost as if the word of His grace is listed as having power to do something. The word is able to build you up! Not only does God build up His people in grace, He also uses means to do this work. But why does Paul commend them to God and particular means? Is God not good enough? Is God not powerful enough? Or could it be that here, among many other places in the Bible, which we will encounter, Paul is saying that God is going to use particular, ordinary means to accomplish His work? If so, as a thirsty believer, I want to know what those means are.

God Uses Means to Grow His People in Grace

This clause, "which is able to build you up," in Acts 20:32, is an interesting one. When we use the phrase "means of grace," my fear is that, because we are using the word "grace," some may think we are saying that something like the preached word, the Lord's Table, or prayer can save us in and of itself; however, that is not the biblical message. Rather, what we mean by this phrase is that God uses these very means as the mechanisms to birth and strengthen saving faith within the believer. It is the Spirit who must work to effectually call a believer through preaching, and it is the Spirit who must work in the means of preaching, sacraments, and prayer for them to be effective. However, we are told within the Scriptures that God works His grace among His people through these ordinary means of grace. In 2 Peter 1:2 we read, "Grace and peace be multiplied to you." I have often thought that this is a statement of great encouragement; in fact, I like to sign emails or letters with these very words, but for many years I was unaware of the greater implication of these words. What does Peter mean by saying "grace and peace be multiplied to you"? Multiplication by definition increases something. So what is increasing? Let's observe what he writes in 2 Peter 1:2-4.

> Grace and peace be multiplied to you in the knowledge of God and of Jesus our Lord, ³ as His divine power has given to us all things that *pertain* to life and godliness, through the knowledge of Him who called us by glory and virtue, ⁴ by which have been given to us exceedingly great and precious promises, that through these you may be partakers of the divine nature, having escaped the corruption *that is* in the world through lust.

What does it mean for grace to be multiplied to a person? When Peter says, "Grace be multiplied to you," he is not saying that a person must continue to be converted over and over again. Rather, he is saying that the Christian, by faith, will come to understand more of, and receive spiritual nourishment through, this grace in increasing fashion. Every bit of the believer's spiritual life is about God's grace. We are justified by God's grace, sanctified by God's grace, and glorified by God's grace. When you and I stand in the new heavens and the new earth, and we sing, "Hallelujah to the Lamb—Worthy is the Lamb," we will be there because Christ took every bit of the penalty that we deserve. That is the good news of the gospel. The gospel is not about human beings trying to do better to earn their standing before God. We do want to be better, but we cannot do it left to ourselves. We are wicked sinners, and the moment that a person places faith in Christ, he is forever changed, redeemed by the blood of Christ, but God does not leave him there. He grows him, nurtures him, and strengthens him in faith and in His word. God has not left us to build-up ourselves, but has delineated several means that He predominately uses to do that. This of course does not mean that they are the only things that He may use in a Christian's life, but He has identified specific, regular, ordinary means that He will use to grow believers in grace.

When we say means of grace, therefore, we are not talking about things that save in and of themselves; rather, we mean the particular ways in which God uses these things to increase His work of grace in those that He has saved. It is a clear distinction that is necessary to make, for it does not mean that the means of grace are able to operate in and of themselves. The means are what the Spirit uses as He works.

Here is one definition of the means of grace that I would like to put forward: *the instruments Christ ordinarily uses to birth and strengthen the faith of the elect as He is present among them.* There are a lot of saints who have gone before me who have written fuller definitions than this one; however, I would like us to use this one as we walk through this primer together.

It is quite possible for the Lord to use anything in the life of a believer. Many could attest to the fact that God often utilizes things outside of the ordinary means of grace; however, there are certain things that He tells us He will definitely use, and that is the main difference. That is why we labeled them the "ordinary" means of grace. They are the things that the Scriptures have said are instituted by Christ through which we can expect blessing, thereby making them a "means of grace."

Church historian and Baptist scholar James Renihan is helpful in delineating the idea that there are many things the Lord uses to strengthen our faith, but that when we say "means of grace," in an historical context, what we are really saying are two things: first, Christ instituted them, and second, that they come with a promise of blessing, or more specifically, we can expect blessing from them.[1] The Bible lists some particular means, or instruments, through which the grace of God is multiplied in the life of the believer. Remember, these means do not justify you more, for justification is a one-time declaration of righteousness before God based on the merits of Christ alone; rather, they are means through which our faith, the grace of faith, is strengthened. It is these means that we must pursue, and when we do in faith, we can expectantly await spiritual blessing.

God Uses Specified Means to Strengthen the Faith of His Covenant People

The Word
The specified means of grace that we see in Paul's commendation to the church at Ephesus is the ministry of the word. Paul speaks to this elsewhere when he discusses how the proclamation of the word is one of the means of grace. Look at Romans 10:14-17.

> How then shall they call on Him in whom they have not believed? And how shall they believe in Him of whom they have not heard? And how shall they hear without a preacher? [15] And how shall they preach unless they are sent? As it is written: "How beautiful are the feet of those who preach the gospel of peace, Who bring glad tidings of good things!" [16] But they have not all obeyed the gospel. For Isaiah says,

---

[1] I commend to the reader a wonderful set of lectures, delivered by Dr. Renihan at the Southern Baptist Founders Conference—Southwest, September 25-27, 2014 at Heritage Baptist Church, Mansfield, TX. These lectures have furthered my thoughts on the ordinary means of grace.

"Lord, who has believed our report?" [17] So then faith *comes* by hearing, and hearing by the word of God.

This passage is saying the ordinary means by which the Lord grants faith and converts sinners is through hearing the word preached. This is the very reason why the dominant thing that we should be offering on Sunday mornings is the ministry of the word. There are a lot of things that the church of Jesus Christ is doing today, but I fear that the major thing that the Lord tells us to use to bring about the saving of souls is what many want to minimize. Often times in churches all throughout the United States, Lord's Day services are intentionally focused on minimizing the preaching of the word and gearing services towards "seekers." However, the word of Christ preached was the focus of the apostles, the early church, and is precisely what the Scriptures command to be central within the church. Faith comes from hearing and Paul says this word is able to build you up. We're in the building business! The ministry of the word, therefore, is one of the means that the Scripture says the Lord uses.

Look again at what Paul says to the Ephesian elders in Acts 20:32, "So now, brethren, I commend you to God [and notice, he chooses one of the means] and to the word of His grace, which is able to build you up and give you an inheritance among all those who are sanctified." In this phrase, "word of His grace," is he talking about the whole Bible, the written word of God, or is he talking about just the gospel? I think the primary focus is on the gospel but the gospel as revealed in the entire Bible. In this context, Paul talks about the actual gospel, the good news of salvation in Christ, but he also talks about how he's labored to teach them everything profitable. Genesis through Revelation is one big story with lots of little stories that make up an overarching narrative. We are to understand, then, that within this text the means he is talking about is the gospel preached, which we can expand then to Holy Scripture itself.

Friend, the word of God is used by the Spirit of Christ to accomplish two things as seen in this text. The first thing that the word of God does is give you an inheritance among all those who are sanctified. And that takes us back to Romans 10, doesn't it? How do you get saved? The Spirit works in your heart, preaches internally to your soul the truthfulness of the gospel, as the preacher is preaching to your ears. The Spirit causes you to be born again (regeneration), and you respond in faith to the Christ of that gospel message. Paul is showing the way that the Lord grants faith. It is through the ministry of the preached word. The first thing that we need to see about the Bible and the Bible preached is that God does something when it is preached and through the preaching of it.

The second thing that the Bible says is that the word builds you up. We can read of that in places like 2 Timothy.

> All Scripture *is* given by inspiration of God, and *is* profitable for doctrine, for reproof, for correction, for instruction in righteousness, [17] that the man of God may be complete, thoroughly equipped for every good work. (2 Tim. 3:16-17)

Paul said at the end of that Acts text, "an inheritance among all those who are sanctified." First Thessalonians 4:3 says that God's will for you is your sanctification — you being set apart to God in His holiness. That's God's will. Then in John 17:17, Jesus, when praying for the disciples and all who will believe in Him through their report, asks the Father to sanctify them in the word — to set them apart unto Himself by the means of the word. The word of God is the means of saving and a means of growing the people of God.

Baptism
Another identified means of grace is baptism. Consider the words of Matthew 28:18-20.

And Jesus came and spoke to them, saying, "All authority has been given to Me in heaven and on earth. [19] "Go therefore and make disciples of all the nations, baptizing them in the name of the Father and of the Son and of the Holy Spirit, [20] "teaching them to observe all things that I have commanded you; and lo, I am with you always, *even* to the end of the age." Amen.

The entire goal of Jesus' commission is the discipleship of believers, which includes not only evangelism, but the ultimate growth of the believer in the things of Christ. Notice that we are commanded to baptize because Christ instituted baptism. His final words to His disciples were essentially that they were to utilize the ministry of the word ("teaching them to observe all that I have commanded you") and baptism. Once again, our two-fold system: Christ-instituted and the promise of blessing. Where's the promise of blessing? It's in verse 20, where the Lord says, "and lo, I am with you." Here, Jesus says that He promises to be with His church as they teach and baptize. His presence *is* the promised blessing.

The Lord's Supper
We have discussed the ministry of the word and baptism, but there is a third means that the Scripture gives us — the Lord's Supper. In 1 Corinthians 10:16, Paul is writing to a church that is confused about many things, and they needed instruction regarding the Lord's Table. Here is what Paul says in the midst of discussing idolatry: "The cup of blessing which we bless, is it not the communion of the blood of Christ? The bread which we break, is it not the communion of the body of Christ?" (1 Cor. 10:16). We will examine this passage closer in a chapter that follows, but allow me to give you a preview here. The apostle is not saying that the Lord's Supper is an act whereby we simply remember Jesus. He is

saying we have fellowship (*koinōnia*) with Jesus, or fellowship in the blood and body of Christ. We know Christ gave us this ordinance to be practiced, and we see here that when we do, there is an expectation of participation, or fellowship, with Christ.

Prayer

All throughout the Bible, the people of God are told to pray, and we see that Christ called His followers to pray. He gives us a model in Matthew 6. In 1 John 5:14, we see the blessing that accompanies prayer: "Now this is the confidence that we have in Him, that if we ask anything according to His will, He hears us." What does it mean to pray according to the will of God? It means to pray with an open Bible given that the Scriptures are God's revealed will to us. Where is the blessing? The blessing is in the identity of the God to whom this verse refers. God hears us when we pray according to His will. We pray to the Father, in the name of the Son. It is because of Jesus' work that we can come to God, and the blessing is that because of the accomplished work of Christ through His death and resurrection, we can pray to the Sovereign of the universe and know that He hears us. It may often feel like our prayers are unheard or go unanswered, but the promise of Scripture is that the God of the universe hears believers when they pray. That is the blessing. There is a promised blessing here that we must cling to as we approach God in prayer.

Summary

God is free to use any means in the life of any believer to grow and strengthen their faith, but the aforementioned means are the primary instruments through which He has told us He will work. This is good news! These means assume a risen, reigning, and present Christ. Christ promises to be present with His church, and unlike the Roman Catholic view of the sacraments, these means alone do not have power to work. They must be accompanied by the work of the Spirit of Christ and by faith on the part of the believer. It is the present reigning of Christ through His Spirit wherein He gives us certain means to strengthen us all the way home. What wonderful news it is that Jesus has not left His church without His presence! Jesus says, "I will build My church, and the gates of Hades shall not prevail against it" (Matt. 16:18).

When we speak of this idea of the ordinary means of grace, we are standing on the shoulders of others that have come before us. Here is what John Calvin writes, when speaking of the Lord's Supper.

All we say is, that God uses the means and the instruments, which he sees to be expedient, in order that all things may be subservient to his glory, he being the Lord and disposer of all. Therefore, as by bread and other aliment [i.e., that which nourishes] he feeds our bodies, as by the sun he illumines, and by fire gives warmth to the world, and yet bread, sun, and fire are nothing, save inasmuch as they are instruments under which he dispenses his blessings to us; so in like manner he spiritually nourishes our faith by means of the sacraments, whose only office is to make his promises visible to our eye...[2]

The Lord is gracious to give us actual, tangible things to remind us of His promise of covenant grace. Here's how theologian Charles Hodge defines means of grace: "Those

---

[2] John Calvin, *Institutes of the Christian Religion*, Book IV, Chapter XIV, Section 12. Taken from John Calvin, *Institutes of the Christian Religion*, trans. Henry Beveridge, vol. II. (Grand Rapids: Eerdmans, 1983), 499.

institutions which God has ordained to be the ordinary channels of grace, i.e., of the supernatural influences of the Holy Spirit, to the souls of men."[3] You see, Hodge is calling the work of the Holy Spirit in your life grace. Therefore, a means of grace is a means or a channel that the Lord uses by the work of the Spirit in your life. To summarize this, God builds up His people in grace, He uses means to do so, and He tells them in the word what those means are.

Late nineteenth- to early twentieth-century Dutch theologian Herman Bavinck defines the means of grace similar to Calvin. He says they are the "...external, humanly perceptible actions and signs that Christ has given his church and with which he has linked the communication of his grace."[4]

We should not be careless in the use of these instruments. We should see them as necessary blessings bestowed to the Christian. By implication, we see that absence from Lord's Day worship is not simply a missing of fellowship, but it is an absence from the ordinary means that the Lord uses in the life of the believer. The ordinary means of grace belong to the church gathered on the Lord's Day. We should also give consideration to how we prepare ourselves for the ordinary means of grace. We should approach each Lord's Day with prayerful expectation of the Lord's work in our lives through these means. These are channels that the Lord uses in our lives — He is active as we come in faith — so, we must consider our own preparation and readiness week in and week out. When we use these means in faith, we are asking God to increase our faith, to

---

[3] Charles Hodge, *Systematic Theology* (Grand Rapids: Eerdmans, 1986), 3:466. Accessed from Thomas R. Schreiner and Matthew R. Crawford, eds. *The Lord's Supper: Remembering and Proclaiming Christ Until He Comes*, Volume 10, NAC studies in Bible & Theology (Nashville: B&H Publishing Group, 2011), 255.

[4] Herman Bavinck, *Reformed Dogmatics, Holy Spirit, Church, and New Creation*, IV, ed. John Bolt, trans. John Vriend (Grand Rapids: Baker Academic, 2008), 4:448.

strengthen us, and to build us up and help our unbelief. We are asking the Lord for His grace in our lives, and that He would multiply it. We are, in a sense, asking Him, "Bless us with your word and with your presence." That is what we are doing when we come in faith to these means—to the preached word, to baptism, to the Table, and to prayer. Let us recall that encounter where a man met with Jesus in the healing of his child in Mark 9. Do you remember his words? Mark 9:24 says, "Immediately the father of the child cried out and said with tears, 'Lord, I believe; help my unbelief!'" May our prayerful approach to the ordinary means of grace be the same.

I played soccer all throughout high school, and thoroughly enjoyed it. Each year, several weeks before the beginning of school, we would have practices in the summer, running for miles and doing sprints and other kinds of training. Following lengthy runs, our water source was a hose attached to a spigot. Let me tell you, I could not wait at the end of one of those runs to get to the hose. Do you know why? It was not that I like hoses, or that I was drawn to the feel of the hose, or that the crisp nature and green color of the new hose that was purchased meant something to me. It was that the hose was a channel for the water, which I desperately needed. In this discussion of the ordinary means of grace, we are not worshiping the Table. We are not idolizing the Bible or the waters of baptism. What we are saying is that the Lord is going to work and He is going to use means. When I was dry and thirsty, I could not wait to get to the hose. It was like I was thinking to myself, "Give me the hose, because when the hose comes, there is going to be cool, crisp water that is going to nurture my parched lips." Similarly today, what you need is to come in faith to the means that the Lord has ordained—His word, His sacraments, and prayer. As dry as you may feel, He has promised you that He is not leaving you alone. And the "hose" through which He is going to grant you more and more and more tastes of the water of His grace, until Christ returns, is the ordinary means of grace.

Study Questions

1. What does the phrase "means of grace" mean?

2. What are the ordinary means of grace?

3. What sets the ordinary means of grace apart from other tools the Lord uses in our lives?

4. What are some Scripture passages that are necessary to consider regarding the means of grace?

5. How important are the ordinary means of grace for Christian living?

2

The Ministry of the Word

Since you have purified your souls in obeying the truth through the Spirit in sincere love of the brethren, love one another fervently with a pure heart, 23 having been born again, not of corruptible seed but incorruptible, through the word of God which lives and abides forever, 24 because "All flesh *is* as grass, And all the glory of man as the flower of the grass. The grass withers, And its flower falls away, 25 But the word of the LORD endures forever." 1 Now this is the word which by the gospel was preached to you. Therefore, laying aside all malice, all deceit, hypocrisy, envy, and all evil speaking, 2 as newborn babes, desire the pure milk of the word, that you may grow thereby, 3 if indeed you have tasted that the Lord *is* gracious. (1 Pet. 1:22-2:3)

Praedicatio Verbi Dei Est Verbum Dei, which means, "The Preaching of the Word of God is the Word of God," was penned in 1562 by Heinrich Bullinger in what has come to be known as the Second Helvetic Confession, one of the many statements of faith that came about during the Reformation. In a time when people were struggling to understand what the place of the word of God was in the life of the people of God and when the church held the word of God in services unintelligible to most people, men like Bullinger upheld that "The Preaching of the Word of God is the Word of God!" This caused a rebirth in the 1500s of questions like: Why preaching? What is the purpose of the ministry of the word? What happens when the word is unfolded? What should the church's placement of preaching be? How important is it in the life of the body for the word to be taught and preached and proclaimed?

First Peter speaks to those very questions and to the place of the ministry of the word. Let's begin by looking at the context from which our passage comes. In this wonderfully rich book, the apostle Peter writes to believers and speaks of the blessing of salvation. He says:

> Blessed *be* the God and Father of our Lord Jesus Christ, who according to His abundant mercy has begotten us again to a living hope through the resurrection of Jesus Christ from the dead... 10 Of this salvation the prophets have inquired and searched carefully, who prophesied of the grace *that would come* to you, 11 searching what, or what manner of time, the Spirit of Christ who was in them was indicating when He testified beforehand the sufferings of Christ and the glories that would follow.... 16 because it is written, "Be holy, for I am holy." (1 Peter 1:3, 10-11, 16)

At the conclusion of this section, Peter connects the reality that those who are recipients of this great grace are called to holiness (v. 16), and by implication, love (v. 22). Notice that the reality of our salvation and the call to holiness are inseparably related. Peter conveys that, because of this salvation, Christians ought to prepare their minds for action (v. 13, "gird up the loins of your mind"), and so, as seen in 1

Peter 1:13-21, pursue holiness. In light of the call to holiness, Peter then moves to a call to love (v. 22, "love one another fervently with a pure heart"). As a result of this great salvation and because of the call to holiness, Christians are to love one another. Following this, he moves into the place of the word among the people of God.

The Word Is a Means of Conversion and a Means of Grace

Peter, in picking up on this long discussion regarding the Christian's salvation, says, "Since you have purified your souls in obeying the truth…" He's writing about obedience to Jesus Christ and obedience to Jesus Christ is synonymous with, or the same as, conversion or being saved. If you are a believer, when you received Christ by faith, you obeyed the message of the gospel proclaimed to you, the message that declares that you are a sinner and you have no hope of eternal salvation. But Christ, through his gospel proclaims to you a message that you must repent of sin and rest wholeheartedly in the perfect life and atoning death of Jesus in your stead. When you obey, meaning, when you receive by faith alone what Christ has done for you, you are saved. Obedience to Christ in verse 22 ("Since you have purified your souls in obeying the truth [i.e., to the gospel, to the word] through the Spirit in sincere love of the brethren") is contextually connected to verse 2: "…according to the foreknowledge of God the Father, in sanctification of the Spirit, for obedience and sprinkling of the blood of Jesus Christ."

In 1 Peter 1:22, salvation is pictured as obedience to the truth. In verse 23, it's pictured as being born again. These are two ways of referring to the same reality — being saved. Look at verse 23, "…having been born again, not of corruptible seed but incorruptible, through the word of God which lives and abides forever..." Words are important. Notice how that is constructed: "having been born again...through the word of God which lives and abides forever..." Notice that the means of being born again is the "word of God." The Spirit is doing the work but the means (medium, mechanism, or channel) that He uses is the ministry of the word. This shouldn't surprise us, though, for this is what Paul says in Romans 10:14-17 when he writes:

> How then shall they call on Him in whom they have not believed? And how shall they believe in Him of whom they have not heard? And how shall they hear without a preacher? 15 And how shall they preach unless they are sent? As it is written: "How beautiful are the feet of those who preach the gospel of peace, Who bring glad tidings of good things!" 16 But they have not all obeyed the gospel. For Isaiah says, "Lord, who has believed our report?" 17 So then faith *comes* by hearing, and hearing by the word of God. (Rom. 10:14-17)

What we see here in this passage is that the ministry of the word is a means of conversion. Christ has ordained that His church, until He returns, preach the word, and it is through the preaching of the word that the Spirit of God converts sinners. The early Particular Baptists said it this way:

> The grace of faith, whereby the elect are enabled to believe to the saving of their souls, is the work of the Spirit of Christ in their hearts, and is ordinarily wrought by the ministry of the Word; by which also, and by the administration of the baptism, and the Lord's Supper, prayer, and other means appointed of God, it is increased and strengthened. (2LCF 14.1)

The ordinary means that the Lord uses in drawing a person unto salvation is the preaching of the word of God. The

Spirit of God is at work through the means of the word rightly preached or proclaimed.

The preaching of the word, however, is not only a converting means, but it is also a continual means of grace in the life of the believer. Look at 1 Peter 2:2 again, where it says, "…as newborn babes, desire the pure milk of the word, that you may grow thereby." On the one hand, the ministry of the word through the Spirit is what converts us, but on the other hand, we are told to "desire the pure milk of the word, that you may grow thereby." The ministry of the word is not just for unbelieving sinners who need to trust in Jesus. The ministry of the word is of continued necessity for the believer as well. Simply put, the word is a means of conversion *and* an ongoing means of grace. Christ has accomplished everything necessary for salvation. He has sent His Spirit to convert the elect and to nourish them until they are with Him, and all of the work of the Spirit is a work of grace. So, the merit of Christ and His accomplishments are the grace conveyed by these ordinary means, and believers are nourished in this grace (i.e., the benefits of Christ) by the ministry of the word. In 1 Peter 1:23, the Scripture is presented as the means of conversion, and in 1 Peter 2:2 it is a means of continual growth in that salvation — the believer's spiritual milk. The words "pure milk of the word," in the context, are referring to the word of God, but this is not the only lesson we learn from this text.

The Word Faithfully Preached
Is Christ Speaking to His People

Notice again 1 Peter 1:23: "…having been born again, not of corruptible seed but incorruptible, through the word of God which lives and abides forever…" The word is pictured as living. A similar image is given in Hebrews 4:12: "For the word of God is living and powerful, and sharper than any two-edged sword." Peter says that this word is not perishable, but imperishable, pointing back to the Old Testament book of Isaiah 40:6 and 8. Note what he says in verse 24: "All flesh is as grass, and all the glory of man as the flower of the grass. The grass withers, and its flower falls away..." He is contrasting here, as Isaiah did, human flesh and the word of God. All flesh is like grass. If your grass is like mine, it withers very quickly. And regardless of its beauty, the flower falls, but the word of God — the word of the Lord — remains.

What are we to do with this passage? Is the preaching of the word just a pastor teaching facts about God? Are we to become only a people of knowledge, and therefore, strive to learn more facts, concepts, and definitions? Peter seems to indicate that there is more for the believer. While proclaiming truths and facts are certainly a part of what the preaching of the word involves, it is, however, more than that; it is a literal means through which Christ speaks to His people.

Now I want us to hold our place here in 1 Peter and look at three other passages. We won't delve deeply into each of them, but I want you to see various texts where the Scripture says that Jesus speaks or Jesus preaches.

The first is John 10:16. Jesus says, "And other sheep I have which are not of this fold; them also I must bring, and they will hear my voice; and there will be one flock and one shepherd." Did you see what Jesus said? Predominantly speaking of the Gentiles, He said, "they will hear my voice." In this context, the Gentiles are portrayed as hearing the voice of Jesus.

The second text is in Acts 26. Listen to Luke's account of Paul before King Agrippa:

"Therefore, King Agrippa, I was not disobedient to the heavenly vision, 20 "but declared first to those in Damascus and in Jerusalem, and throughout all the region of Judea, and *then* to the Gentiles, that they should repent, turn to God, and do works befitting repentance. 21 "For these reasons the Jews seized me in the temple and tried to kill *me*. 22 "Therefore, having obtained help from God, to this day I stand, witnessing both to small and great, saying no other things than those which the prophets and Moses said would come— 23 "that the Christ would suffer, that He would be the first to rise from the dead, and would proclaim light to the *Jewish* people and to the Gentiles." (Act 26:19-23)

Note where Paul says that "Christ...would proclaim light to the *Jewish* people and to the Gentiles." We will come back to this.

Let's look at one more text. Recall that, in Ephesians 2, Paul is writing to the church at Ephesus saying that two peoples, Jews and Gentiles, have been brought together, and that God has now taken down the wall that divided the two through the gospel. Paul writes that salvation comes to us by grace through faith and not works (Eph. 2:8-10). In Ephesians 2:13-16, he says:

> But now in Christ Jesus you who once were far off have been brought near by the blood of Christ. 14 For He Himself is our peace, who has made both one, and has broken down the middle wall of separation, 15 having abolished in His flesh the enmity, *that is*, the law of commandments *contained* in ordinances, so as to create in Himself one new man *from* the two, *thus* making peace, 16 and that He might reconcile them both to God in one body through the cross, thereby putting to death the enmity.

Notice Ephesians 2:17, where we read, "And He came and preached peace to you who were afar off and to those who were near." We must ask ourselves, when did Jesus literally come and preach to the Gentile Ephesians? Jesus didn't ever go in the flesh and preach to these Ephesians during His earthly ministry. The resurrection and ascension happened long before most of the Ephesians had even heard the message of Christ. So when did Jesus come and speak to these Gentiles? When did they hear Christ's voice? Recall John 10:16. As when Paul said in Acts 26 that Jesus preached light to the Gentiles and again in Ephesians 2:17 that Jesus came and preached to the Ephesians,[1] could it be that, in these texts and others like them, the Scripture is saying that when the message of Christ is faithfully proclaimed, Christ is proclaiming a message?

You see, as the preacher faithfully proclaims the word, Christ speaks through the Spirit to bring about conversion and to grow His sheep. Something happens when the word is preached. Listen to early Particular Baptists on this issue from the Baptist Catechism. This was written in 1693.

> *Q. 94: How is the Word made effectual to salvation?*
> A. The Spirit of God makes the reading, but especially the preaching, of the Word, an effectual means of convincing and converting sinners, and of building them up in holiness and comfort, through faith, unto salvation.[2]

Again, we want to be clear, it is God doing the work, but the means or mechanism He uses is the preached word. So, essentially, we can say Christ is preaching. As Paul said to the Ephesians, "He came and preached peace to you," meaning that they heard the word of God and as they did, Christ was speaking through His word. So when Jesus said in John 10:16, "My sheep hear my voice," he was not

---

[1] I am indebted to Dr. James Renihan for connecting the dots on this passage for me.

[2] *The Baptist Confession of Faith & The Baptist Catechism* (Birmingham, AL: Solid Ground Christian Books; Carlisle, PA: Reformed Baptist Publications, 2010), 116.

referring to some kind of mystical experience where we think, "I need to listen for an audible voice in my head." What He meant was that the word that the Spirit has given through the prophets and apostles is His final revelation, and as it goes forward, He will be preaching, converting, feeding, and nurturing people until they are with Him face to face. The preaching of the word of God is the word of God.

Now, it needs to be said that we do not mean that the preacher himself has any value in and of himself in this regard, or that he becomes one with God. But we can say that insomuch as a preacher stands in a pulpit and preaches the Scriptures, having faithfully studied and now interpreting, exegeting, and proclaiming the word of God, that it is the word of God to the people of God. I hope you saw that there were a lot of variables there, because there is a lot of what passes for preaching on television, in conferences, or in churches all across this globe today that is not the word of God. And in those cases, we cannot say that this so-called preaching is the word of God, for the person delivering the sermon is not actually proclaiming the authoritative counsel of the Lord. But when God's word is rightfully proclaimed, Christ speaks to His people, which is why we call it the word of Christ.

So, let's return to 1 Peter. Look at what Peter says next in verse 25, quoting from Isaiah: "'But the word of the LORD endures forever.' Now this is the word which by the gospel was preached to you." This message is the message of the gospel, but it's more than that; all of Scripture is really, ultimately, the message of Christ. In the same context, Peter will say, "desire the pure milk of the word." This word is the saving work of Christ, the covenantal work of Christ, the glory of God among the nations, the singular message from Genesis to Revelation. The word that was proclaimed to you, and as Isaiah and 1 Peter say, and as we can affirm on the authority of Scripture, this word of God remains forever. So, yes, Peter is referring to the gospel message, but ultimately to Christ revealed in all the Bible.

Do you remember that account of what happened on the road to Emmaus? In Luke 24 we read the record of two disciples who had followed Jesus but, shortly after His resurrection, had not yet heard the news that He had been raised. Jesus appeared to them, but they did not recognize Him. He converses with them, and we read in Luke 24:27 the following words of Luke: "And beginning at Moses and all the Prophets, He expounded to them in all the Scriptures the things concerning Himself." Did you catch that? Jesus was saying that Moses and the Prophets are about Him. Oftentimes many think, "Well, Jesus doesn't show up until the New Testament," but that is wrong. Jesus has always been the overarching theme that ties Genesis to Revelation together. This is why "He expounded to them in all the Scriptures the things concerning Himself."

You see, a faithful preacher is simply a mouthpiece through which God speaks. Something happens when the word is faithfully preached. It is a means of conversion, it is a means of grace, and, as it is faithfully preached, Christ speaks to His people. This draws us to a third and final consideration in this chapter.

The Word Is the Centerpiece of the Ministry of the Church

This is a crucial point. I think most of us would assume this, but let's examine it for a minute. Look at the instruction in 1 Peter 2:1-2, where we read, "Therefore, laying aside all malice, all deceit, hypocrisy, envy, and all evil speaking, as newborn babes, desire the pure milk of the word, that you may grow thereby..." There is a clear reference to the word of God. It is the means through which the Spirit brings about new birth, and it is the food that feeds the people of God on their journey home. However, the text says that we are to "desire" it, "that you may grow thereby." Notice that the focus is ultimately that of spiritual growth. We can see this on the surface, but what does it mean? There is a sense in which the salvation of the Christian was fixed and yet, God can say through Paul in His word, "work out your own salvation with fear and trembling" (Phil. 2:13). Similarly, Peter admonishes here a growth in the salvation that one has in Christ.

There is another way to say it. Conversion assumes an interest and delight in the things of God. Conversion, salvation, being born again or regenerated, and going from darkness to light, all assume an interest and delight in the things of God. Ultimately salvation is tasting of the goodness of God in our souls, and if you've tasted of it, you'll grow. This is not to say that we earn or accomplish our salvation, but simply that truly saved people grow in their faith. The knowledge of Christ and the means of our growth in Him come from the word of God, and therefore the word is the centerpiece of the ministry of the church.

So, are you discouraged? Perhaps you have not read the Bible in two or three weeks. If so, go right to the cross and proclaim the gospel to your heart with repentance and pray, "Lord, tomorrow; morning, evening, lunchtime, whenever it is, give me the ability to just eat one or two verses of Your food." Conversion assumes an interest and delight in the things of God. Peter's words echo Psalm 34:8, where we read, "Oh, taste and see that the LORD is good!" This reminds us of what Paul said to the Ephesian elders, doesn't it? Recall Acts 20:32, which we previously discussed, "So now, brethren, I commend you to God and to the word of His grace, which is able to build you up and give you an inheritance among all those who are sanctified." In other words, Paul commends them to the word, not only as a converting means, but as means of grace which is able to build them up.

All of this brings us to a very practical question: What is the place of the preaching of the word of God in the true churches of God? The ministry of the word must be the centerpiece of the church, because it is through the word of Christ that we are initially converted by the Spirit and through the word of Christ that we are subsequently nourished in that faith. Therefore, we must understand that the central time of our weekly rhythm is the preaching of the word.

On the final pages of the Bible, we are given a glimpse of Christ standing among His churches (Rev. 1:13) and giving each of them His word. It is this same Christ who stands among His churches today, leading them through His word. What believers need today is the voice of this One who is described in the following way:

> Then I turned to see the voice that spoke with me. And having turned I saw seven golden lampstands, 13 and in the midst of the seven lampstands *One* like the Son of Man, clothed with a garment down to the feet and girded about the chest with a golden band.
> 14 His head and hair *were* white like wool, as white as snow, and His eyes like a flame of fire; 15 His feet *were* like fine brass, as if refined in a furnace, and His voice as the sound of many waters; 16 He had in His right hand seven stars, out of His mouth went a sharp two-edged sword, and His countenance *was* like the sun shining in its strength. (Rev. 1:12-16)

The voice of Christ is what people need!

Study Questions

1. How is preaching a means of grace?

2. How does Ephesians 2:17 inform our understanding of the ministry of the word?

3. Why must preaching be central in the local church?

4. How does preaching as an ordinary means of grace change our understanding of Christ's work among His church?

3

Baptism:
Sign of Covenant
Membership

And Jesus came and spoke to them, saying, "All
authority has been given to Me in heaven and on
earth. ¹⁹ "Go therefore and make disciples of all the
nations, baptizing them in the name of the Father
and of the Son and of the Holy Spirit, ²⁰ "teaching
them to observe all things that I have commanded
you; and lo, I am with you always, *even* to the end of
the age." Amen. (Matt. 28:18-20)

In these final words to the apostles, Jesus instructs them to
baptize disciples in the name of the triune God. He tells
them that as they do, He promises His presence with them
until the end of the age. Now, we know that churches who
claim the name of Christ down through the ages have a
variety of ways of looking at this text, and indeed, the entire
theology of baptism. There are those who believe that the act
of baptism at the first few days of an infant's life starts the
process of salvation. There are others who stress baptism as
so uniquely connected to the work of regeneration that they
are almost one and the same, if not the same. Then there are
churches that teach baptism should be given to members of

a household led by believing parents. Finally, there are those who insist that baptism should be solely reserved for those who are understandingly professing faith in the covenant love and salvation of God. What is clear is that Jesus tells all the faithful down through the ages to baptize in the triune name.

God has assigned to His church, in His word, specific means whereby He nourishes and strengthens her faith. I agree with many of the Reformers that baptism is one of those means. Notice these words from 1693 that Baptists included in their catechism:

> Q. 93: What are the outward means whereby Christ communicateth to us the benefits of redemption?

Observe what they said; not saves us, but communicates, or grants us, the benefits of our already accomplished salvation. Here is the actual wording of the answer:

> A. The outward and ordinary means whereby Christ communicateth to us the benefits of redemption are His ordinances, especially the word, baptism, the Lord's Supper, and prayer; all which means are made effectual to the elect for salvation.

But they go further:

> Q. 96: How do Baptism and the Lord's Supper become effectual means of salvation?
> A. Baptism and the Lord's Supper become effectual means of salvation, not for any virtue in them, or in him that doth administer them, but only by the blessing of Christ, and the working of the Spirit in those that by faith receive them.

This describes what the earliest Particular Baptists (forebears to Confessional Reformed Baptists today) believed and points to the idea, contained within the Great Commission, of Christ being with His disciples as they baptize. Jesus promises to be with His church down through the ages as they baptize in the triune name.

Four Crucial Points about Baptism

At this point, we should note four crucial points about baptism.

The act of baptism does not save anyone.
The first reality is that the act of baptism does not save anyone. The view that it saves is known as baptismal regeneration. There are people who believe that baptism starts the process, or in some cases is the sum total of the process of salvation. But the Scripture says that we are saved by grace through faith, not of works, including outward religious works. So baptism does not save in and of itself.

Baptism is a command of Christ.
Another aspect, which we have seen already, is that baptism is a command of Christ. Jesus institutes baptism as an ordinance, or sacrament, of His church, which is to be practiced. Therefore, it is right that we seek to understand it, both in its practice and in its benefit, given that our Lord has commanded that we, His followers, observe it. To summarize so far, baptism does not save, and yet Jesus commands that it be done.

Baptism belongs to the church.
A third truth is that it was a practice of the early church and it belongs to the church. This idea is one about which we need to be clear. Baptism was an ordinance, or a sacrament, that was given to the church. It was not given to a parachurch organization. It wasn't given to individual

persons who perhaps decide one day to start baptizing others, or to baptize his or her own self. Baptism was given by Christ to His apostles and therein to His church. It was a practice of the early church. Let me give one such example to you. You can see this in Acts 2:41. Peter preaches a wonderful sermon, laying out the gospel, and then the final part of the description of what happened is this: "Then those who gladly received his word were baptized; and that day about three thousand souls were added *to them*." This is the beginning of the description of the church in Acts. God has always had an assembly, or covenant people, from the very beginning—but the New Testament church is beginning to practice baptism as a sign of the new covenant. We can read of Paul's baptism in Acts 9, or of Lydia's baptism in Acts 16, as well as that of Cornelius. Baptism then, was a practice of the early church, and in addition to the clear command of Christ to observe it, we can, by right understanding of the Scriptures, infer that we are to do it as well, given its apostolic example.

Baptism is a one-time observance.

Finally, the fourth insight that we need to make clear is that baptism is a one-time observance. The Lord's Supper is a continual sacrament, or ordinance, that should be practiced regularly. Baptism, however, is a one-time event. We do not baptize an individual every time he decides that he feels like he needs to be closer to God. Prescriptively, within the Scripture, we see that baptism is a one-time ordinance whereas the Lord's Supper occurs regularly. And as a person surveys the Scriptures, he sees that baptism is actually mentioned in a multitude of places. There may be a common misconception that it is infrequently mentioned, but it really shows up often within the pages of the New Testament.

Baptism: Ordinance or Sacrament?

I have been using the words "ordinance" and "sacrament" interchangeably. Perhaps you come from a tradition where ordinance, something that's ordained, is the only word used. Or maybe in your tradition the word sacrament is used. I tend to agree with those scholars, pastors, and teachers who see those words as being able to be used interchangeably. Though we can use those terms interchangeably, it is important to distinguish them. Technically speaking, "ordinance" refers to that which has been ordained by Christ. "Sacrament" refers to what an ordinance is in terms of what it does when blessed by the Spirit of Christ: that is, it is a means of grace. In short, whichever word we use, we mean the two visible signs that Christ commanded to His church with the assumption of blessing, and baptism is indeed one of those things.

A sacrament points to something we need to remember. We often think about sacraments beginning in the New Testament, but God has always given His people visible signs that remind and proclaim His word visibly, or in a tangible way. Adam and Eve were given two trees. Noah was given a rainbow. Abraham was given circumcision. Since the death, burial, and resurrection of Christ, those visible signs that the Lord has given to His church are baptism and the Lord's Supper. We call them signs because they are not just things that we do, but rather they are the word of God in visible form.[1] When we come to the Lord's Supper and the bread is broken, that is the word of God proclaimed to us in tangible form announcing again that the body of Christ was broken for us. It is a visible sign for our eyes of the word of God, specifically the promise of the

---

[1] It appears that Augustine was one of the first to use the phrase "visible word" (Augustine, *Contra Faustum*, 19.16). I am appreciative to Dr. Samuel Renihan for furthering my thoughts on this idea of "visible word."

gospel of Jesus Christ. So, too, baptism is a word made visible, and as such it is a means of grace. Sacraments, or ordinances, are signs that point to something, and when we observe them, God is proclaiming His word through them. I do not mean that we should listen closely for an audible voice. What I mean is that the message of Christ and the covenant of grace are proclaimed, yet delivered in a tangible, visible form.

Baptism is not just something we perform to celebrate that someone is not going to go to hell. That is a true reality of the salvation that Christ brings. However, there's more to baptism than just celebrating that little Johnny has gotten saved. Now to make that case, we need to walk through the New Testament and see just how often the apostles want us to consider our own baptism. I am going to make the argument that when we observe a baptism within our own local churches, it is not just for the person being baptized. Rather, it is for the benefit of the whole church. Specifically, as someone is lowered into the water and raised to walk, symbolically, in newness of life, each of us has the ability to reflect on our own baptism. Our baptism then becomes a sign again and again and again that the Lord uses to nurture us in our faith. It is a means of grace. It is a sign that points to something. And to illustrate that, I am going to walk us through the New Testament.

Baptism as a Means of Grace

Let's look at how the New Testament regularly calls believers to remember their own baptism and see therein four specific truths about this instrument of grace.

It is a sign proclaiming union with Christ.
If we were traveling on any road today, we would see signs that point to specific locations. These road signs are crucial

for us, but they are not the destination themselves. For instance, the road sign that says "Philadelphia" is not Philadelphia, but it points to Philadelphia. Similarly, baptism is a sign, which points the way to something. It proclaims union with Christ. We can see this in at least two different passages. First, in Romans 6, the word of God says:

> What shall we say then? Shall we continue in sin that grace may abound? 2 Certainly not! How shall we who died to sin live any longer in it? 3 Or do you not know that as many of us as were baptized into Christ Jesus were baptized into His death? 4 Therefore we were buried with Him through baptism into death, that just as Christ was raised from the dead by the glory of the Father, even so we also should walk in newness of life. (Rom. 6:1-4)

If that was the only passage of Scripture that we had, we might begin to think that baptism itself is what saves us. But remember, we must interpret the Scripture by the Scripture, and we cannot form any doctrine based on one single verse, taking it out of its connection to the rest of Scripture, or we could make the Bible say just about whatever we want it to say. This text is saying that when a Christian is baptized, it is a picture, a sign, of his or her union with Christ. Jesus' death has become that person's death. So, when you feel guilty over the sins that you committed this past week, for instance, remember that Jesus died for those sins, and your baptism is a reminder that when Jesus died, you died.

Baptism is a sign, which proclaims union with Christ, but Paul does not just tell the church at Rome that. He also tells the church of Colossae in Colossians 2.

> In Him you were also circumcised with the circumcision made without hands, by putting off the body of the sins of the flesh, by the circumcision of

Christ, [12] buried with Him in baptism, in which you also were raised with *Him* through faith in the working of God, who raised Him from the dead. [13] And you, being dead in your trespasses and the uncircumcision of your flesh, He has made alive together with Him, having forgiven you all trespasses, [14] having wiped out the handwriting of requirements that was against us, which was contrary to us. And He has taken it out of the way, having nailed it to the cross. (Col. 2:11-14)

God's judgment concerning you is "guilty," but through faith, God's penalty for that guilt is to punish, to cut off, someone else in your place, namely, Jesus. Just as in the physical act of circumcision there is a cutting away, similarly, Jesus was cut off in the place of the believer. It is now the circumcised heart of the believer that is the replacement for the old covenant sign of circumcision. Just as in the Abrahamic covenant there was a sign (i.e., circumcision) pointing to a promise, so under the inaugurated new covenant there is a sign of the gospel promise of grace. Baptism is the sign which proclaims union with Christ. The Scripture does not give us the idea that the act of baptism as an act itself is what buries us. Rather, the Holy Spirit is what connects us to the work of Christ, but baptism is a sign which proclaims our union with Christ.

When a baptism occurs, those of us who have been baptized can certainly celebrate with the person being baptized. But there is more for us. We can remember, too, that we have received the sign of the covenant of grace, whereby we have been buried with Christ. We should not view baptism as a celebration of what we have done, but a proclamation of what God has done and our connection to it through faith. As a Reformed Baptist pastor, I have often encouraged my congregation during a baptism to reflect on their own baptism and confession of faith in Christ, not as a celebration of their response to God, but upon God's covenant promise to them. Understood rightly, baptism is a covenant sign. It declares God's promise to save all who come to Him in faith. Baptism, then, is a sign that portrays union with Christ. Paul, in two different places, uses baptism to picture this reality.

It is s sign preaching new life.

A second thing is this: baptism is a sign which preaches new life. Did you know that when someone is baptized in the assembly of believers that it is a visible sermon? Listen to what Paul says in that same passage in Romans 6:

> What shall we say then? Shall we continue in sin that grace may abound? 2 Certainly not! How shall we who died to sin live any longer in it? 3 Or do you not know that as many of us as were baptized into Christ Jesus were baptized into His death? 4 Therefore we were buried with Him through baptism into death, that just as Christ was raised from the dead by the glory of the Father, even so we also should walk in newness of life. (Rom. 6:1-4)

Baptism does not just point to the fact that the believer is united with Christ in His death, but also that he or she is united with Christ in His life. And there is a two-fold aspect to that. Right now, Christian, you have spiritual life that you didn't earn. It was granted to you based on the merits of Christ, applied to you by the Spirit of Christ. But that life doesn't end when you die. Just like Christ was raised, you, too, will be raised. So, baptism is a sign, which preaches new life. Jesus' resurrection provides for our life now and our life to come. But Paul doesn't just say that in Romans. Look at what he writes in Galatians 3:27, which says, "For as many of you as were baptized into Christ have put on Christ." Many of you know that in some of the New Testament books there is a tension that Paul exposes which is the idea of "putting off" and "putting on." In Galatians 5, we see the fruit of the Spirit, and we see a discussion of things that do not exhibit this fruit (drunkenness, orgies, rivalry, etc.). We don't work the spiritual fruit up in ourselves, rather, the Spirit of God, as He is sanctifying us using the means of God, causes that fruit to exist in our lives. Baptism is a reminder not only of our union with Christ, but it also preaches new life to us. When a person is baptized, that individual is getting a non-verbal sermon from God, and we as the congregation are also getting a message. Christian, when you come in faith to Christ, you have new life, and baptism points to that new existence, which Christ has wrought. Baptism *is* a celebration that someone has "gotten saved," but it is much more. Why else would the apostle Paul constantly tell the people to remember their baptism by how he uses it as a sign pointing to spiritual realities?

It is a sign pointing to a community.

A third truth we see in the Scriptures is that baptism is a marker that points to connectedness with the body of Christ. Just like we should not observe the Lord's Supper by ourselves, but rather with the body, baptism also serves as a reminder that we are part of a body. Notice what Paul writes to the church at Ephesus in Ephesians 4:

> *There is* one body and one Spirit, just as you were called in one hope of your calling; 5 one Lord, one faith, one baptism; 6 one God and Father of all, who *is* above all, and through all, and in you all. (Eph. 4:4-6)

There is one body of Christ and one Spirit of Christ. This is essentially what he's saying, and he's using all of these reminders: one Lord, one faith, one baptism. The same apostle says it this way in 1 Corinthians 12:

For as the body is one and has many members, but
all the members of that one body, being many, are
one body, so also *is* Christ. [13] For by one Spirit we
were all baptized into one body—whether Jews or
Greeks, whether slaves or free—and have all been
made to drink into one Spirit. (1 Cor. 12:12-13)

It is as if Paul cannot stop using the sacrament of baptism to
regularly jog the memories of the people to whom he writes.
And so baptism becomes a reminder to our call to a unity
which Christ forges. He brings people into His body, His
bride, by virtue of it being His. And Paul uses the idea of
baptism as a sign to talk about that unity. In fact, he uses
baptism in another way to talk about unity. Look at 1
Corinthians 1, where Paul is writing to a needy, broken
church:

Now I plead with you, brethren, by the name of our
Lord Jesus Christ, that you all speak the same thing,
and *that* there be no divisions among you, but *that*
you be perfectly joined together in the same mind
and in the same judgment. [11] For it has been declared
to me concerning you, my brethren, by those of
Chloe's *household*, that there are contentions among
you. [12] Now I say this, that each of you says, "I am of
Paul," or "I am of Apollos," or "I am of Cephas," or
"I am of Christ." [13] Is Christ divided? Was Paul
crucified for you? Or were you baptized in the name
of Paul? [14] I thank God that I baptized none of you
except Crispus and Gaius, [15] lest anyone should say
that I had baptized in my own name. [16] Yes, I also
baptized the household of Stephanas. Besides, I do
not know whether I baptized any other. [17] For Christ
did not send me to baptize, but to preach the gospel,
not with wisdom of words, lest the cross of Christ
should be made of no effect. (1 Cor. 1:10-17)

In a discussion on unity, where does he go? The singular sign of the entrance of people into God's community — baptism. There is a sense in which when we baptize someone we are saying that that person belongs to the body of Christ. Paul essentially says that in addition to union with Christ and new life in Christ, baptism also points to the connectedness that a Christian has to the church.

It is a sign giving assurance.

In many churches over the last few hundred years, baptism has been jettisoned as a continual reminder of certain promises, specifically in times of wrestling with assurance. However, baptism in the New Testament was meant to be a once-for-all sign that constantly points the baptized person to the realities that he needs to consider in times of weak assurance; namely, the promise of God. Unfortunately, in many church contexts, a sinner's prayer or aisle-walk at an invitation has become what churchgoers have been instructed to look back on. We have taken baptism from its rightful place and sort of added it as a tack on. In no way do I doubt that sinners crying out to God for the first time in faith and repentance are saved. What I am saying, however, is that baptism is the real sign the Lord has given His people as a continual reminder of the promise of His covenant. Therefore, "remember your baptism" is an appropriate phrase for the believer. By appropriate I do not mean that baptism is what saves a person, but that it points that person back to the promises of the One who saves.

Peter refers to baptism this way in 1 Peter 3:

> For Christ also suffered once for sins, the just for the unjust, that He might bring us to God, being put to death in the flesh but made alive by the Spirit, [19] by whom also He went and preached to the spirits in prison, [20] who formerly were disobedient, when once the Divine longsuffering waited in the days of Noah,

> while *the* ark was being prepared, in which a few, that is, eight souls, were saved through water. [21] There is also an antitype which now saves us — baptism (not the removal of the filth of the flesh, but the answer of a good conscience toward God), through the resurrection of Jesus Christ, [22] who has gone into heaven and is at the right hand of God, angels and authorities and powers having been made subject to Him. (1 Pet. 3:18-22)

Admittedly, this text has been variously interpreted and presents some challenges. I think that Peter discusses baptism in connection with the Old Testament story of the ark, specifically in the sense that there was in Noah's day a call to repentance. Similarly, baptism is a mechanism which God gives to the church, not in and of itself to clean people, but a sign to return to as an appeal to God. It is an appeal, a pledge to God, "the answer of a good conscience toward God" based on God's promise.

For a long time in many churches, we have forgotten that baptism is a sign. We need to discover again the robust theology of baptism. Baptism is something that God has given to us to remind us that we have been buried with Christ and raised to walk in new life. Every time you see a baptism, you indeed offer praise to the Lord for His saving work in the life of others, but you also can "remember your baptism" as a sign that the Lord has given you to remind you of His covenant of grace and all that that means for you. Don't forget that Peter says baptism is "the answer of a good conscience toward God." What could that verse mean if all we do with baptism is think about it the day that we got baptized? How is it an "answer of a good conscience"? Is it just a short-term thing? Or is it Peter telling the church to reflect back on their own baptism, and that when they think upon it, and see that sign being enacted, that it is a reminder to them of the promises of the God who saves — the God who brings people through the waters of judgment, just like He brought those eight safely through the flood in Noah's ark? He is the God who brings the elect home through the work of Jesus Christ.

I think there are several examples in day-to-day life that can help us here. For instance, you often hear people say things like: "That cholesterol check saved my life" or "That EKG saved my life." They are thankful for the test that told them something. However, the test was not the lifesaver, but the remedy was. The test merely pointed to something. Or, for instance, consider those signs in a building that direct you to an exit. The sign doesn't save you in the event of an emergency evacuation, the actual exit does. The sign just points to what actually saves you. Peter is not saying that water saves you. He is saying that baptism is a sign that points to the One who does. And notice the verb tense used here. Peter is writing to believers. He calls them elect exiles and he is using the present tense to talk about an action in the past. How could he not mean for them to think about their baptism? We may have other reminders of God's saving work such as a date written in our Bible, or the story of an evangelistic crusade wherein we came to know the gospel. By all means, continue to rejoice in those memories. However, look to the main sign that the Lord has given you to continue to recall His saving promise. Baptism is a sign that we are called to remember over and over again.

Conclusion

Over the last few years, I have truly rejoiced as a pastor who baptizes new believers. I will often remind them that their baptism is a sign of God's covenant promise and that we can look together to His promise in Christ. Far too often in my life, even as the one administering the ordinance, I missed the opportunity for God's sermon, the visible word proclaimed in the sacrament of baptism, to be preached to my heart. And what is the content of that sermon? It tells us that through faith we are united with Christ and that we have new life in Him. It also proclaims to us that we have communion in His body and that we have a regular sign that helps us with assurance, pointing us to the truths of the gospel. And it is a means of grace, because through it God confirms our faith, both the faith of the one who is receiving baptism as well as all those in the body of Christ who are a part of that day. Recall the words of our Lord, where Matthew tells us He says:

> All authority has been given to Me in heaven and on earth. 19 Go therefore and make disciples of all the nations, baptizing them in the name of the Father and of the Son and of the Holy Spirit (Matt. 28:18b-19)

We also read in Acts 8 the amazing story of the Ethiopian eunuch who was reading from Isaiah as he rode in his chariot. Following a discussion of the gospel of Jesus Christ from the Old Testament Scriptures, the eunuch was baptized and as the Scriptures say in Acts 8:

> So he commanded the chariot to stand still. And both Philip and the eunuch went down into the water, and he baptized him. 39 Now when they came up out of the water, the Spirit of the Lord caught Philip away, so that the eunuch saw him no more; and he went on his way rejoicing. (Acts 8:38-39)

I can guarantee you that this would not be the only day this eunuch would think about his baptism. We dare not miss the visible sermon that is proclaimed in this beautiful means of grace.

Study Questions

1. What is baptism?

2. How is it a means of grace?

3. What are some truths that are proclaimed in baptism?

4. When baptism occurs as a part of Lord's Day worship, how might the entire congregation benefit?

4

The Lord's Supper: Feast of the Covenant

And as they were eating, Jesus took bread, blessed and broke *it*, and gave *it* to them and said, "Take, eat; this is My body." 23 Then He took the cup, and when He had given thanks He gave *it* to them, and they all drank from it. 24 And He said to them, "This is My blood of the new covenant, which is shed for many. 25 "Assuredly, I say to you, I will no longer drink of the fruit of the vine until that day when I drink it new in the kingdom of God." (Mark 14:22-25)

Meals are a regular occurrence in our lives. We eat, sometimes alone, but often with others. It is during these occasions that our bodies receive vital nourishment to continue on and make it to the next meal. God has designed our bodies such that we need regular nourishment through the intake of food in order to live and move forward for His glory. Sometimes, however, there are meals that have a communal connection, or perhaps even a ceremonial flavor. One can think of the great meals of the average person's life such as a wedding dinner, an anniversary date, a governmental state dinner, or an annual Thanksgiving. It is in these times that the participants are not only nourished, but there is a celebration around a table of an important event, often times including specific promises that have been made. It is to these meals that most of us turn to later on as great memories remembered with fondness.

The Old Testament people had such a meal. Annually, in the celebration of the Passover as their physical bodies were nourished, the redemption God had granted from slavery in Egypt was celebrated. This feast involved not only the intake of food, but also a remembering of the blood of a slaughtered Lamb, which was a marker of those who were gloriously saved from judgment. This annual feast was a highpoint of their year as, each time, gathered around the table with covenant family, the freedom God had granted was commemorated and His continued covenant promise was proclaimed. It was a meal that fed and proclaimed a message. It was in the celebration of this meal recorded for us in Mark 14 that Jesus chose to institute a new covenant meal known as the Lord's Supper. For the Christian, the covenant promise of God is heralded as the participant is fed spiritually upon the body and blood of Christ, as He is spiritually present among them. Therefore, this meal is a means of grace.

Three Truths about the Supper as a Means of Grace

I want us to see three truths about this meal as a means of grace. Specifically, this is a meal that proclaims or preaches covenant blessings to those coming in faith, it is a meal whereby the Person of Christ is uniquely present with His people, and it is a meal whereby the faith of the participant is strengthened and increased.

This is a meal of covenant blessings.
The text in Mark 14 points us to the words of Jesus as He instituted the Lord's Supper. Specifically, in pointing to the cup, He refers to it as "the blood of the covenant." In other

Gospel passages, Jesus was further recorded as saying that it was the new covenant in His blood (Matt. 26:28 and Luke 22:20). Just like the old covenant people, we too have a feast whereby the freedom that God has granted to us is proclaimed and whereby we simultaneously are nourished in His promise. The Lord brings each of His people into the covenant of grace, a covenant through which the merits of His Son are imputed to the sinner, and the atrocious sinful record of the sinner is done away with by the blood of Christ, and all of God's free grace. This covenant was promised from Genesis 3:15 and is founded in the trinitarian arrangement known as the covenant of redemption. A confessional statement on this is most helpful:

1. The distance between God and the creature is so great, that although reasonable creatures do owe obedience to him as their creator, yet they could never have attained the reward of life but by some voluntary condescension on God's part, which he hath been pleased to express by way of covenant.

2. Moreover, man having brought himself under the curse of the law by his fall, it pleased the Lord to make a covenant of grace, wherein he freely offereth unto sinners life and salvation by Jesus Christ, requiring of them faith in him, that they may be saved; and promising to give unto all those that are ordained unto eternal life, his Holy Spirit, to make them willing and able to believe.

3. This covenant is revealed in the gospel; first of all to Adam in the promise of salvation by the seed of the woman, and afterwards by farther steps, until the full discovery thereof was completed in the New Testament; and it is founded in that eternal covenant transaction that was between the Father and the Son

about the redemption of the elect; and it is alone by the grace of this covenant that all the posterity of fallen Adam that ever were saved did obtain life and blessed immortality, man being now utterly incapable of acceptance with God upon those terms on which Adam stood in his state of innocency. (2LCF 7)

It is this very covenant that the Lord's Supper proclaims. When the Christian takes the Lord's Supper, the covenant of grace is being declared again in all its wonder to those who come in faith. It is the blessings of this covenant that the recipient once again has an opportunity to lay hold of as the sign of the Lord's Supper is given. The seventeenth-century English Baptist Benjamin Keach said:

There is a mystical conveyance or communication of all Christ's blessed merits to our souls through faith held forth hereby, and in a glorious manner received, in the right participation of it.[1]

Visibly, the promise of God to save all who come by faith in Christ is announced. When we partake in the Lord's Supper, the covenant promise of God, the God who never changes (Mal. 3:6), is preached to our hearts and to the assembly gathered around the table. Thus, the Lord's Supper is a covenant meal — a covenant feast.[2]

The presence of Christ is here.
A debate throughout the history of the church has been about the nature of the Lord's Supper. Many have argued

---

[1] Benjamin Keach, *Preaching from the Types and Metaphors of the Bible* (Grand Rapids: Kregel Publications, 1972), 639.

[2] I refer the reader to my work, *A Covenant Feast: Reflections on the Lord's Table* (Pittsburgh: Ichthus Publications, 2016) for a more lengthy treatment on this.

that God actually grants salvific, justifying grace through the operation of the meal. Some have claimed that the bread and wine actually change into the literal body and blood of Jesus Christ. Others have denied these things and have said nothing supernatural occurs in the Lord's Supper, but rather, it is only a memorial of the sacrifice of Jesus. However, counter to these varied beliefs, some have professed, and rightly I believe, that while the bread and wine do not change in any way at the Supper, Christ is spiritually present with His people in a special way at the table. It is this view that I believe is the most biblical understanding of the meal of communion.

The Puritan confession of the early Particular Baptists reads:

> Worthy receivers, outwardly partaking of the visible elements, in this sacrament, do then also, inwardly by faith, really and indeed, yet not carnally and corporally but spiritually, receive and feed upon, Christ crucified, and all benefits of His death: the body and blood of Christ being then, not corporally or carnally, but spiritually, present to the faith of believers in that ordinance, as the elements themselves are to their outer senses. (2LCF 30.7)

Notice that in the Mark 14 text, Jesus refers to the connection between the bread and His body, and between the cup and His blood. This is not an argument for a literal relationship, but it is also not so symbolic that a connection between the two items can't be made. Rather, as 1 Corinthians 10:16 declares, when we partake of the Lord's Supper, we have communion or fellowship (*koinōnia*) with the body and blood of Christ:[3] "The cup of blessing which we bless, is it not the communion of the blood of Christ? The bread which

---

[3] I strongly encourage the reading of Richard Barcellos' *The Lord's Supper as a Means of Grace: More than a Memory.*

we break, is it not the communion of the body of Christ?"(1 Cor. 10:16).

In 1 Corinthians 10:16, contrasting pagan sacrifices (as participation with demons) with the Lord's Supper (as participation in the body and blood of Christ), Paul reminds the early Corinthians believers, and all Christians down through the ages, that participation in the Lord's Supper is an eating of literal bread and a drinking of literal wine, but it is also a spiritual participation in the body and blood of Jesus. Thus, while the elements do not change, we have spiritual fellowship with the present Lord. Sinclair Ferguson says it this way:

> It is not by the church's administration, or merely by the activity of our memories, but through the Spirit that we enjoy communion with Christ, crucified, risen, and now exalted. For Christ is not localized in the bread and wine (the Catholic view), nor is he absent from the Supper as though our highest activity were remembering him (the memorialist view). Rather, he is known through the elements, *by the Spirit*. There is a genuine *communion* with Christ in the Supper. Just as in the preaching of the Word he is present not in the Bible (locally), or by believing, but by the ministry of the Spirit...so he is also present, in the Supper, not *in* the bread and wine, but by the power of the Spirit. The body and blood of Christ are not enclosed in the elements, since he is at the right hand of the Father (Acts 3:21); but by the power of the Spirit we are brought into his presence and he stands among us.[4]

The word "communion" in 1 Corinthians 10:16 is the Greek word for fellowship (*koinōnia*) and it is fellowship not

---

[4] Sinclair B. Ferguson, *The Holy Spirit* (Downers Grove, IL: InterVarsity Press, 1996), 201.

with other people that is primarily in view, but rather fellowship with Christ and the effects of gospel work that are in view. So, each time you come in faith to the Lord's Supper, Christ is spiritually present with you in a unique way. Of course, He always promises to be with us down through the ages (Matt. 28), but in a particular way, at the Supper, we commune with Christ through the Holy Spirit. Seventeenth-century Dutch theologian Wilhemus á Brakel ruminates on this same idea this way:

> ...we must reflect upon the matter *signified* in the Lord's Supper. The signs have not been instituted for the purpose of serving God by partaking of them, for God is a Spirit who must be served in a spiritual matter. These external signs conceal spiritual matters. Christ has instituted bread as a sign and symbol of His body, and the breaking of it as a sign of the breaking of His body by His suffering and death... When seeing these signs, the communicant must not end in them mentally, but must proceed to the matter signified, that is, to the body and blood of Christ — broken and shed to satisfy God's justice for the sins of believers. Thus, he must unite the sign to the matter signified.[5]

Spiritual nourishment is made available.
Various confessional or catechetical statements help to bring together what the Scripture teaches regarding the Lord's Supper; specifically, it is of particular value to the spiritual nourishment of the Christian who attends to the Supper in faith. Notice these helpful statements:

> The grace of faith, whereby the elect are enabled to believe to the saving of their souls, is the work of the

---

[5] Wilhemus á Brakel. *The Christians Reasonable Service*, vol. 2, ed. Joel R. Beeke, trans. Bartel Elshout (Grand Rapids: Reformation Heritage Books, 2015), 532.

Spirit of Christ in their hearts, and is ordinarily wrought by the ministry of the Word; by which also, and by the administration of baptism and the Lord's supper, prayer, and other means appointed of God, it is increased and strengthened. (2LCF 14.1)

...that Christ has commanded me and all believers to eat of this broken bread, and to drink of this cup, and has joined therewith these promises: First, that His body was offered, and broken on the cross for me, and His blood shed for me, as certainly as I see with my eyes the bread of the Lord broken for me, and the cup communicated to me; and further, that, with His crucified body and shed blood, He Himself feeds and nourishes my soul to everlasting life as certainly as I receive from the hand of the minister, and taste with my mouth, the bread and cup of the Lord, which are given me as certain tokens of the body and blood of Christ. (Heidelberg Catechism, Question 75)

Given that the Lord's Supper is a visible proclamation of covenant promises and that it is a time of unique fellowship with Christ, the above-mentioned confessional and catechetical statements are right in viewing the Lord's Supper as an ordinary means of grace whereby the people of God are nurtured. This nourishment is a spiritual provision, wherein the faith of the believer is increased. As we have already seen, in biblical covenants, God has given His people visible signs, which point to His promise within that covenant. The new covenant is no different and indeed is the ultimate covenant where this reality reaches its fullest expression. In the Lord's Supper, the word of God is proclaimed to the people of God, and they are edified in the grace accomplished and secured by their Savior.

Often, many Christians treat the Lord's Supper as only an occasional occurrence where they think about the death of Jesus, but it is so much more. A visible sermon is heralded, and the Holy Spirit ministers the spiritual presence of Christ to the faithful participant. Oh what a joy, believer! Our souls are fed and our faith is nourished as we partake of this meal. What a feast, and what a Savior who does everything necessary to grant you a seat at the table. Christian, this is more than just a time to think about the cross; it is a very real feast with Jesus — a feast where your very faith is enriched, strengthened, and increased!

Study Questions

1. What is the Lord's Supper?

2. How does the Supper strengthen and increase the faith of the participants?

3. What does it mean that Christ is present among His people at the Supper?

4. What does proper preparation for the Supper look like?

5

The Means of Grace of Prayer

Seeing then that we have a great High Priest who has passed through the heavens, Jesus the Son of God, let us hold fast *our* confession. 15 For we do not have a High Priest who cannot sympathize with our weaknesses, but was in all *points* tempted as *we are, yet* without sin. 16 Let us therefore come boldly to the throne of grace, that we may obtain mercy and find grace to help in time of need. (Heb. 4:14-16)

We have been observing the ordained means that God has given through which the merits of Christ's once-for-all redemption are more and more beneficial in the life of the believer. Prayer is also one of the ordinary means that the Lord uses.

An Overview of Prayer as a Means of Grace

Fervent prayer marked the early church. In Acts 2:42, we are given a beautiful picture, which reads: "And they continued steadfastly in the apostles' doctrine and fellowship, in the breaking of bread [I believe this to be a reference to the

Lord's Supper] and in prayers." Many scholars say that that phrase "and in prayers" seems to indicate that they were praying known prayers, but it could simply indicate that they were regularly in prayer together, and that there was regular time of corporate prayer. I prefer the latter meaning. The early church was devoted to prayer. Later in Acts 12:5 we read, "Peter was therefore kept in prison, but constant prayer was offered to God for him by the church." A chapter later, in Acts 13, we come upon these words:

> Now in the church that was at Antioch there were certain prophets and teachers: Barnabas, Simeon who was called Niger, Lucius of Cyrene, Manaen who had been brought up with Herod the tetrarch, and Saul. 2 As they ministered to the Lord and fasted, the Holy Spirit said, "Now separate to Me Barnabas and Saul for the work to which I have called them." 3 Then, having fasted and prayed, and laid hands on them, they sent *them* away. 4 So, being sent out by the Holy Spirit, they went down to Seleucia, and from there they sailed to Cyprus. (Acts 13:1-4)

The Holy Spirit sets apart men for the work of the church, but we see the church also prays and sets these men apart. Fervent prayer marked the early church in all that it did.

Now why was prayer so important in the early church? Well, the Lord Christ Himself ordained prayer. One of the things we have mentioned is that when we say something is a means of grace, there are two things that we indicate. One of them is that Christ ordained it. Even though prayer was occurring prior to the earthly ministry of Christ, we read in the New Testament a command of Christ to pray. For instance, in John 16, Jesus spoke about the time that would come after His resurrection. There we read:

> And in that day you will ask Me nothing. Most assuredly, I say to you, whatever you ask the Father

in My name He will give you. 24 Until now you have asked nothing in My name. Ask, and you will receive, that your joy may be full. (John 16:23-24)

Jesus tells us that if we want joy, we should ask. And, who can forget Jesus' instructions in Matthew 6:9, "In this manner, therefore, pray: Our Father in heaven, Hallowed be Your name."

The Lord Himself told His followers to pray. The early church was marked by what Jesus said to do—to pray. But not only is prayer a means of grace that the Lord instituted, it is a means of grace because there is an expectation of blessing when we do it, just like the ministry of the word and the sacraments.

Look at a few related passages. In John 14:13-14, Jesus says: "And whatever you ask in My name, that I will do, that the Father may be glorified in the Son. If you ask anything in My name, I will do *it*." There is an assurance of blessing in prayer. Our experience may feel like we have been praying and our words do not get higher than the ceiling as if there is no blessing coming, but Jesus qualifies it, doesn't He? There is an expectation that when the child of God prays, God will receive glory.

In 1 John 5, the apostle John writes:

Now this is the confidence that we have in Him, that if we ask anything according to His will, He hears us. 15 And if we know that He hears us, whatever we ask, we know that we have the petitions that we have asked of Him. (1 John 5:14-15)

One of the covenantal blessings that you and I have as the covenant people of God and one of the assurances that we have as children of God, is that God hears us. This is a blessing in and of itself. The God who created all things, the triune God who saves wretched sinners and bids them come, the God who is in control over every single molecule that exists, hears us. This God makes Himself known to His covenantal people as the God who hears them. So why is prayer a means of grace? Because Christ has said do it and there is an expectation of blessing. We are going to talk about this word "blessing" in a little while, for we are not to assume that we can expect everything according to our will. But at this point, let us say that prayer, like the ministry of the word, is a means of grace because Christ has said do it and that command is accompanied with a promise of blessing.

Hebrews 4:16 and Prayer as a Means of Grace

Now let's look at Hebrews 4, specifically verse 16, which says, "Let us therefore come boldly to the throne of grace, that we may obtain mercy and find grace to help in time of need." Now there may be some skeptical readers who will think, "Grace to help in time of need? Really?" Many could list all the circumstances that did not go the way they desired when they prayed, and yet there is a promise here: "come boldly...that we may obtain mercy and...grace."

Let's pick apart this verse. The first thing we need to observe in Hebrews 4:16 are the first three words: "Let us therefore." These words bid us to ask a prior question as to what the basis is for our confidence to draw near. The answer is given for us in verses 14-15, where we read:

> Seeing then that we have a great High Priest who has passed through the heavens, Jesus the Son of God, let us hold fast *our* confession. 15 For we do not have a High Priest who cannot sympathize with our weaknesses, but was in all *points* tempted as *we are, yet* without sin. (Heb. 4:14-15)

The writer of Hebrews, focusing on the gospel, says because of Jesus we can pray with confidence. But what does it mean, "who has passed through the heavens…"? Jesus died for sin, but on the third day He rose. His resurrection is certainly about Jesus' coming to life again, but it was also about the reality of Christians having a hope in their own resurrection to come. It is the confidence of every Christian that, when we stop breathing and are placed into the ground and our soul goes to be with the Lord, there will come a day when our bodies will be raised because our Savior was raised. This Jesus is the one who, after His resurrection, has passed through the heavens. Jesus' placement, then, at the Father's right hand is not because God has a forgetful memory, but serves as a pledge to all of us that we have a true hope in Christ that is secure.

Not only do we have Christ's shed blood to cover our sin, but Christ was tempted so He understands weakness. This does not mean that He was weak in temptation, for He never sinned. If Jesus would have sinned, He would not have been blameless and thus He could not have been the mediator between God and man. Yet, because He was tempted, we have a great high priest who understands and sympathizes with His people.

In verse 16, the Greek word for "boldly" connotes courage, boldness, or fearlessness. Jesus is our confidence. You see, when we pray, whether we feel guilty in confession, or feel weary, or lack faith, our assurance is not in ourselves, but is in Christ. The writer of Hebrews wants us to grasp that. Look, when you pray a few weary phrases to the God of the universe, He hears, but He hears because of Jesus who is not weak and who is not lacking in anything. Don't pray with the assumption that you don't have enough faith to come to God. If you are a Christian, you have everything necessary to assume that the God of the universe will hear you.

Consequently, as the passage says, "Let us therefore come boldly to the throne of grace…" The assumption is that you already have saving grace, so I do not think this is an evangelistic passage. This is a letter to believers who are seeking to follow God. So the call here to "come boldly" is to move close to God, and how do we do that? We go to God in prayer. Now that's not to say when it says "come boldly" other means of grace are not included. The implication is "Let us then pray." We have confidence and boldness to pray. That verb is in a tense in Greek that signifies ongoing action, which could be rendered as follows: "Let us continue to come boldly," or "Keep on drawing near." We have confidence because of the finished work of Christ. A few verses later in Hebrews 7:25 the writer says, "Therefore He [Jesus] is also able to save to the uttermost those who come to God through Him, since He always lives to make intercession for them." One of the roles of Jesus as our high priest is that He makes intercession for His people.

Since we are told to draw near, unto what do we draw near? We are told to draw near to the throne of our Savior whose very enthronement offers us mercy and grace. As the ruling and reigning King, He continually offers grace and mercy to His people from His throne. The word "grace" is connected with "to help in time of need." What you and I need in times of need is grace. That phrase could literally be translated "a timely help."

I hope that you can see thus far that Christ has told us to pray, that there is the expectation of blessing, and the writer of Hebrews conveys the idea that, because of what Christ has done, who Christ is, and where He is, we have every confidence to pray. Therefore, prayer is one of the ordinary means of grace. Notice what the writer of Hebrews says: "Come boldly, so that you receive grace." Do you see that in this text? The Christian is invited to draw near unto God in order to receive grace.

I have labored here to make the case that prayer is a means of grace because so often we don't think about it that way. If we really considered that prayer is a means of grace, what might we do? Pray fervently? Pray more? Pray more deliberately? Pray with others with more frequency? Observe what Paul tells the Ephesian Christians in Ephesians 3.

> For this reason I bow my knees to the Father of our Lord Jesus Christ, 15 from whom the whole family in heaven and earth is named, 16 that He would grant you, according to the riches of His glory, to be strengthened with might through His Spirit in the inner man, 17 that Christ may dwell in your hearts through faith; that you, being rooted and grounded in love, 18 may be able to comprehend with all the saints what *is* the width and length and depth and height— 19 to know the love of Christ which passes knowledge; that you may be filled with all the fullness of God. (Eph. 3:14-19)

Essentially, Paul is praying for the growth, encouragement, and spiritual nourishment of the Ephesian believers. As Paul prays, he has in view the edification of this people. His plea with the Lord is that those for whom he prays would further know the enthroned Christ and all that He is for them. Paul, then, understands his prayers for them to be a means through which this change comes.

How often do we seek to be the means of grace for someone rather than using the means of grace for someone? At least that is my temptation. When there is a problem, my first response is to say that I am going to fix it. Or for others, "How can I help you? Your car's broken down? I'm going to come hold the flashlight while you work on it." There is nothing necessarily wrong with wanting to help others. In fact, in the early church, we see much helping ministry occurring among the believers. But sometimes the best thing that we can do is to remember that God has told us that if we pray, He hears, and what a great hope that is. The Scripture demonstrates this truth in many places.

Three Ways in Which We Are to Pray

Keeping all of this in mind, let us look to the Scripture and see at least three ways in which we are to pray.

We are to pray in the name of the Son.
You and I do not have the hope of prayer outside of a mediator. Now I am not saying that if one day you pray and forget to voice the phrase, "In Jesus' name," then you won't be heard. But it glorifies God when we pray in Jesus' name. Those words are not magical, ritualistic words that will cause God to listen. Rather, we pray with the recognition that we are coming through the second Person of the Trinity. We need to understand that we are to pray in and through Jesus. John 14:13-14 says, "And whatever you ask in My name, that I will do, that the Father may be glorified in the Son. If you ask anything in My name, I will do it." Christ is the One through whom we pray. Saying something in Jesus' name is not a way of manipulating God. Instead, we pray in Jesus' name because it is through Him that we have access to God. Every prayer that the Christian prays is essentially a continual reminder that our very approach to God is only through a mediator. When we pray, we have an opportunity to trumpet the truths of the gospel. Jesus' work on our behalf grants us the open door to God. So we see in this text that we are to pray in the name of the Son.

We are to pray according to the Father's will.
We live in a day when many contend that they claim things—material, earthly things—believing that God will grant them based on their demand. It is one thing to believe and trust a promise of God. It is entirely different to tell God with selfish or divided heart motives what you expect Him to give you. What does it mean, then, to pray according to the will of God? First, notice 1 John 5:14-15.

> Now this is the confidence that we have in Him, that if we ask anything according to His will, He hears us. [15] And if we know that He hears us, whatever we ask, we know that we have the petitions that we have asked of Him.

Part of the blessing of prayer (we talked about how prayer is a means of grace because there is a blessing attached to it) is that we have the opportunity to speak to God. Here, in this passage of Scripture, we have the promise that God hears believers. It is a blessing simply knowing that God promises to hear.

But this text, among others, helps us to see that we do not get to dictate to God what God is going to do. Let me explain this. The question is often asked as to whether prayer changes the mind of God. We must be clear to say that God does not change His mind. God reveals Himself, His nature and attributes, as unchanging. Malachi 3:6 says, "For I am the LORD, I do not change." We also understand that God decrees all things that come to pass. Notice the following confessional summary of the truth of Scripture:

> God hath decreed in himself, from all eternity, by the most wise and holy counsel of his own will, freely and unchangeably, all things, whatsoever comes to pass; yet so as thereby is God neither the author of sin nor hath fellowship with any therein; nor is violence offered to the will of the creature, nor yet is the liberty or contingency of second causes taken away, but rather established; in which appears his wisdom in disposing all things, and power and faithfulness in accomplishing his decree. (2LCF 3.1)

We might be tempted then to ask why we should bother to pray. The answer is that when we pray the revealed will of God in faith, we have God's word that it will be done. Look at 1 John 5:14: "Now this is the confidence that we have in Him, that if we ask anything according to His will, He hears us." I do not think it's too bold to say, when you pray the revealed will of God in faith, you have God's word that it will be done. So what does that mean if prayer does not change God's mind? Ultimately, we need to pray with an open Bible, for the will of God is clearly revealed in His word. We should pray the will of God as revealed in the Scriptures. For instance, 1 Thessalonians 4:3a says, "For this is the will of God, your sanctification..." When you and I sincerely pray in faith something like the following, "Lord, sanctify me," He will do it. Why? Because He said it is His will, and in such a prayer we are praying the will of God. Another example might be Matthew 6:9, where we read, "In this manner, therefore, pray: Our Father in heaven, Hallowed be Your name." We are told to pray that the name of God will be hallowed in our hearts. When we pray according to this revealed will, the Lord will do it.

I want to build the case that we are called to pray in faith and that we pray according to the will of God as we pray according to the Scriptures. Now there are going to be times when we do not know what God's will is in a situation. Perhaps you might be thinking, "But what about that verse in James — the prayer of a righteous man availeth much? You just said prayer does not change God's mind, but the text in James 5 seems to say that my prayer changes God's mind." Well, let's look then at James 5.

> Is anyone among you suffering? Let him pray. Is anyone cheerful? Let him sing psalms. 14 Is anyone among you sick? Let him call for the elders of the church, and let them pray over him, anointing him with oil in the name of the Lord. 15 And the prayer of faith will save the sick, and the Lord will raise him up. And if he has committed sins, he will be forgiven. 16 Confess *your* trespasses to one another, and pray

for one another, that you may be healed. The effective, fervent prayer of a righteous man avails much. [17] Elijah was a man with a nature like ours, and he prayed earnestly that it would not rain; and it did not rain on the land for three years and six months. [18] And he prayed again, and the heaven gave rain, and the earth produced its fruit. (James 5:13-18)

The context of this verse is the Old Testament story of Elijah from 1 Kings 18. Basically, God told Elijah that there would be rain (1 Kings 18:1), and yet, Elijah prays, "Lord, bring rain." And what does God do? He brings rain. Elijah prays according to the revealed will of God. The lesson of James, then, is seen in Elijah, the man of faith, as he prays according to the revealed will of God, and God answers that prayer accordingly.

So, we pray in Jesus' name and we pray according to the Father's will. But there is one further element of importance for us.

We are to understand prayer as Spirit-aided communion with God.

A pivotal thing that we need to understand about prayer is that in it we commune with God with the help of the Holy Spirit. The means of grace and the Holy Spirit are connected. We often forget the third Person of the Trinity, but without Him we would be utterly lost. What do I mean by communing with God and praying with the Spirit's assistance? Look at what Scripture says in Romans 8.

Likewise the Spirit also helps in our weaknesses. For we do not know what we should pray for as we ought, but the Spirit Himself makes intercession for us with groanings which cannot be uttered. (Rom. 8:26)

Maybe you are thinking to yourself that, indeed, you want to pray more and with greater quality, but often times you do not even know what to pray. Suffice it to say, the Spirit intercedes for us, particularly as we pray, aiding our prayers and giving to them something than we cannot. The Lord is active in our prayers, and we are never alone in the praying process.

When we think about prayer, we must realize that we are called to do it. It is a means of grace. We are to pray in the name of the Son, and we are to pray according to the Father's will, which assumes that we want to grow in understanding the Father's will. One way to know the Father's will is to just look at His commands. Perhaps it is one of the Ten Commandments that we are praying through in confession or in a desire to grow in holiness and obedience. Maybe we are praying through a passage in the New Testament which speaks of the fruit of the Spirit or what the Bible says about love in 1 Corinthians 13. Be reminded and encouraged that we are aided in our prayers as we pray the revealed will of God in His written word.

Praying for Issues Not Revealed in Scripture

Perhaps you are wondering how you might pray for specific needs that are not clearly outlined in the Scriptures. For instance, maybe it is the uncertainty of how to pray for a family member who has cancer. As you pray, make your request to God, realizing that you do not know the ultimate will of God for the given situation since it has not been revealed like other things (e.g., one of the Ten Commandments as part of the preceptive will of God). Prayer for needs is not a matter of claiming an outcome, but rather it is professing trust in the God of the outcome. Often, our prayers tend to be about results. "Lord, please, cause there not to be cancer." Now I do not think that this is an ungodly prayer. But I would just encourage us to consider praying for more than that. Perhaps our prayer should more often sound something like this: "Lord, no matter what happens in this situation, Your will be done. Would You bring patience and longsuffering and love and joy and peace and self-control in this circumstance for this person who has cancer?"

Am I actually suggesting that, as we pray for a believing loved-one who has cancer, we pray for their sanctification and growth in patience? Yes, for it is the revealed will of God for them. Pray it. There's no need to stop praying for physical healing. God often heals from disease, and we should trumpet that. We have a God who heals. But God doesn't always remove every illness in this earthly life. We may ask for healing, but we pray ultimately that the will of God would be done in each and every situation for which we pray.

Paul gives himself as an example of this and does this very thing in 2 Corinthians 12. We are not exactly sure about all of the details of the situation for which Paul prays, but he basically says that the Lord gave him a physical thorn for a spiritual reason. Look at what he says in 2 Corinthians 12.

> And lest I should be exalted above measure by the abundance of the revelations, a thorn in the flesh was given to me, a messenger of Satan to buffet me, lest I be exalted above measure. 8 Concerning this thing I pleaded with the Lord three times that it might depart from me. 9 And He said to me, "My grace is sufficient for you, for My strength is made perfect in weakness." Therefore most gladly I will rather boast in my infirmities, that the power of Christ may rest upon me. 10 Therefore I take pleasure in infirmities, in reproaches, in needs, in persecutions, in distresses, for Christ's sake. For when I am weak, then I am strong. (2 Cor. 12:7-10)

Inherent to that "therefore" of verse 10 is the reality that God did not take the thorn away. If the apostle Paul can have some kind of adversity that God has given to him for a spiritual reason to sanctify him, we could experience the same. So pray. Pray for the weak one. Pray for the sinner. Pray for the sick. Perhaps it may look like this: "Lord, in Jesus' name, I pray that if it is Your will, You would bring physical healing now. But Your will be done. Father, bring sanctifying graces to this person through this particular trial. I cannot see what you are doing, God, but would You do it?" Or perhaps like this: "Father, for this wayward child, would You somehow bring him to Yourself. Yes, I pray that You would remove these circumstances from his life, but Father, bring him...bring him to Your Son." And on and on and on it goes.

A Word about Corporate Prayer and the Public Amen

One thing we should understand is not only that we are to pray as individuals, but we are to pray corporately, too, with the body of Christ. The early church prayed as a body, and the Scriptures reveal that congregations are to pray (Acts 2:42; 12:5; 13:1-4; and 1 Tim. 2:1ff.). Related to this is one of the things that we need to recover, not just during preaching, but during corporate praying. It is the corporate "amen." Read what Paul says in 1 Corinthians 14:16. The context here is Paul's correction of the corporate worship of the church. He is specifically addressing the intelligibility of the language of prayers within the assembly. "Otherwise, if you bless with the spirit, how will he who occupies the place of the uninformed say 'Amen' at your giving of thanks, since he does not understand what you say?" (1 Cor. 14:16). The word "amen" means "Let it be so," or "truly," or "yes." When the church gathers to pray, one of the best things we can do is to listen with our ears and pray along in our minds with the person who is taking his turn in voicing his prayer. The amen said to prayers is a way of agreeing together as the Lord is sought in each and every moment of the prayer. Corporate prayer shown in the Scriptures is an apostolic pattern that we are to follow, and it demonstrates not only the usefulness of prayer, but also the fact that it is a means of grace that the Lord has given His church to be pursued by both individual believers and the assembled body alike.

Closing Words

We return to Hebrews 4 as we close. "Let us therefore come boldly to the throne of grace, that we may obtain mercy and find grace to help in time of need" (Heb. 4:16). In Scripture, we are instructed to pray through Christ, according to the will of God, and when we do not know His will, our prayers ought to be "may God's will be done." And as we have seen, we do not pray by ourselves, for the Spirit intercedes for us as we pray. All the while, we must keep in mind that prayer is sometimes the means the Lord uses to accomplish His will, as the story of Elijah in 1 Kings reveals.

Prayer is a channel of grace. Let us draw nigh then in prayer. In closing, look at Proverbs 8. May this be our reflection as we consider the means of grace of prayer. This is God speaking:

> Blessed is the man who listens to me, Watching daily at my gates, Waiting at the posts of my doors. 35 For whoever finds me finds life, And obtains favor from the LORD; (Prov. 8:34-35)

Do you long to get into the gates of the Lord? Do you want to sit at His door? His very word is there. Are you feeling like you do not know how to pray? Open up the Scriptures.

Pick a passage, noting its context, then ask the Lord for His revealed will to be done. I think we will find when we arrive in the new heavens and the new earth that one of the chief ways the Lord grew us in our faith was through prayer. What if He increases and strengthens our faith by not granting all that we ask for in prayer? Sometimes in saying no to some of our prayers, He grows our faith and trust in Him through the means and process of prayer. Prayer indeed is a blessed means of nourishing the saints on the road of salvation.

Study Questions

1. What is prayer?

2. How is prayer a means of grace?

3. How ought we to pray?

4. How has the Lord used prayer in your life to grow you in His grace?

6

The Green Pastures of Our Shepherd

Therefore I also, after I heard of your faith in the Lord Jesus and your love for all the saints, 16 do not cease to give thanks for you, making mention of you in my prayers: 17 that the God of our Lord Jesus Christ, the Father of glory, may give to you the spirit of wisdom and revelation in the knowledge of Him, 18 the eyes of your understanding being enlightened; that you may know what is the hope of His calling, what are the riches of the glory of His inheritance in the saints, 19 and what *is* the exceeding greatness of His power toward us who believe, according to the working of His mighty power 20 which He worked in Christ when He raised Him from the dead and seated *Him* at His right hand in the heavenly *places*, 21 far above all principality and power and might and dominion, and every name that is named, not only in this age but also in that which is to come. 22 And He put all *things* under His feet, and gave Him *to be* head over all *things* to the church, 23 which is His body, the fullness of Him who fills all in all. (Eph. 1:15-23)

As we close our brief journey together through the ordinary means of grace, we are reminded that the people that God saves through the work of Jesus, He continues to feed through the accomplishments of Christ by the ordinary means of grace. We have seen from the beginning that these means do not save us; rather, they are instruments used for the believer's spiritual nourishment. Ephesians 1:15-23 helps to set the stage for further understanding the means of grace. This passage declares to us that Christ is currently ruling and reigning, even now, over His church, and that He walks among His people (cf. Rev. 1).

As Christians, we are looking forward to a day when we will be face to face with the Lord Christ, but we need not wait for that day to understand that Christ is spiritually present with His church right now. Look at the text in verses 19-20. Paul, praying for this group of Christians, wants them to understand:

> ...what *is* the exceeding greatness of His power toward us who believe, according to the working of His mighty power [20] which He worked in Christ when He raised Him from the dead and seated *Him* at His right hand in the heavenly *places*

This is what the church celebrates every Sunday. We celebrate that Christ died for sins but that He did not remain in the grave. He was raised, and the power of God in raising Christ is also the power of God in seating Christ at the right hand of the Father (v. 20). Notice the language tense there. Christ *is* seated *now*. But what does that mean for us?

Observe how the text continues: "...far above all principality and power and might and dominion, and every name that is named, not only in this age but also in that which is to come." There is no ruler, dictator, president, king, queen, monarch, or regent that is outside of the hand of Almighty God. Every one of them is under the rule, reign, power, and dominion of Jesus Christ, however they may act. Often we read this text and fix our minds on the age to come. But observe what this text says: Christ is seated *now* in power in *this* age.

Then in verse 22, this seated, ruling, and reigning Christ is described in a particular way: "And He put all *things* under His feet, and gave Him to be head over all things to the church." What is the biggest gift that God has given to His covenant people? Why the seated, ruling, reigning, and present Christ! The church then is the body of Christ (v. 23) with Christ as its head. This is necessary for understanding the ordinary means of grace because if we look at the actions that occur in worship, such as the preaching of sermons, baptism, the Lord's Supper, and prayer, and view them as if we are sheep groping in the darkness until we die and see Jesus, then we will misunderstand them. But if we see that even now, given to the church of Jesus Christ is a ruling and reigning and present Shepherd, who feeds His sheep in green pastures, then we will begin to understand that while the preaching of the word, baptism, the Lord's Supper, and prayer do not save us, they are the means that Christ uses as a present Lord. They are the means that Christ, our gifted Head, uses to pasture His flock in this age. We have to understand that the means of grace are predicated, or based upon, the idea that Christ is spiritually present with His church even in this age.

Christ, very God and very Man, is enthroned in heaven. His physical body, like ours, yet already glorified, is with God, but through the Holy Spirit, Christ is present among us. Even though we cannot see Him with our eyes or hear Him with our ears, He is present. This reality becomes the basis for understanding what it means for this present Christ (not this absent Christ) to shepherd and feed His people.

So, how does He do that? Well, of course there can be any number of tools that the Lord uses in our spiritual journey with Him, but the Bible tells us that it is the ordinary means of grace that this present Christ normally uses. Just as a shepherd feeds his sheep, so this Shepherd feeds us. With that in view, I want us to look specifically at the food, the rhythm, and the fence that our Shepherd uses to pasture His sheep until we are all home together.

The Food that the Lord Gives

The thrust of this little book has been that if these things are the avenues that the Lord Christ, through the Spirit, has given to His church to use, then we should pursue them. Oh friend, pursue the food that the Lord gives through given means. Let's remember again what Paul says to the church and to Christians gathered there in Acts 20:32, "So now, brethren, I commend you to God and to the word of His grace, which is able to build you up and give you an inheritance among all those who are sanctified..." See again what he states about that word: it "is able to build you up" — it is a means that the Lord uses to edify. So by the phrase "ordinary means," we do not mean that the Lord only uses a handful of things or that the means themselves are ordinary in that they lack a special reality, rather we mean that these are the things that Christ has ordained to regularly use to bless His people. Christ has set forth things in His word wherein He promises to grow His people when they attend to those very things in faith. Let's review.

First of all, we spoke of the ministry of the word. Peter says this in 1 Peter 2, "as newborn babes, desire the pure milk of the word, that you may grow thereby, if indeed you have tasted that the Lord *is* gracious" (1 Pet. 2:2-3). We are to long for the word like a baby longs for milk. What does milk do for infants? It causes them to grow — it is food. The ministry of the word (the preaching of the word, the reading of the word, and I would say, secondarily, the singing and confessing and praying of the word) is a means that the Lord uses to nurture His people. And remember, this Lord is present. He is not absent as His word goes forth among His people.

Not only is the word something that the Lord uses in the life of His people, He also uses the sacraments and prayer. The two ordinances, or sacraments, that the Lord has given to His church are the word in visible form. We see the word unfolded with our senses and we taste the promises of that word when we come to the Table. Bread and wine do not save us, but they remind us of the message of Christ, the Christ who does save us. We looked at baptism and we saw how the apostles imply that Christians are to consider their baptism. One place is Colossians 2:11-14.

> In Him you were also circumcised with the circumcision made without hands, by putting off the body of the sins of the flesh, by the circumcision of Christ, 12 buried with Him in baptism, in which you also were raised with *Him* through faith in the working of God, who raised Him from the dead. 13 And you, being dead in your trespasses and the uncircumcision of your flesh, He has made alive together with Him, having forgiven you all trespasses, 14 having wiped out the handwriting of requirements that was against us, which was contrary to us. And He has taken it out of the way, having nailed it to the cross. (Col. 2:11-14)

Christian, when you are wrestling with what it means to follow Christ, or when you are struggling with sin, or when you are struggling with doubt, go back to the covenant promises signified in your baptism. Again, this does not mean that your baptism saved you, or that you should elevate the act of baptism above the promises or the Lord of that baptism; rather, it is a picture that God gives you to proclaim all of the glorious truths in Scripture. It is given for His covenant people.

In verses 12 and 13 of Colossians 2, Paul says, "buried with Him in baptism, in which you also were raised with

Him through faith in the working of God, who raised Him from the dead. And you, being dead in your trespasses and the uncircumcision of your flesh, He has made alive together with Him, having forgiven you all trespasses." Do you see, that this is gospel truth, friend? The gospel is not that we earn good standing with God. The gospel is that we cannot merit good standing with God because no amount of works takes away the debt that we owe and, being lost in spiritual death, even the good things that we do are tainted with sin. The gospel is very much what Paul says to the church at Colossae—God forgives our trespasses because of the work of someone outside of us, who is our Lord Jesus Christ. In verse 14, Paul says, "having wiped out the handwriting of requirements that was against us, which was contrary to us. And He has taken it out of the way, having nailed it to the cross."

So one of the means that the Lord gives the church is baptism, and every time we see a baptism, we see unfolded before our eyes the very promises of God contained in His word. But God in His faithfulness and love does not just give us the one sign of the covenant of grace in baptism; He gives us another, which is the Lord's Supper.

We looked in our journey at the Lord's Supper as a means of grace through various passages. We considered 1 Corinthians 10 in particular. There we read the following words: "The cup of blessing which we bless, is it not the communion of the blood of Christ? The bread which we break, is it not the communion of the body of Christ?" (1 Cor. 10:16). As we worked through the Lord's Supper in detail, one of the observations that we made specifically from this text is that when we come to the Lord's Table, our present Lord blesses us spiritually with His presence in a unique way. Is Christ always with His church, according to Ephesians 1? Yes. But when we come to the Lord's Table there is a participation that occurs in the blood of Christ and the body of Christ, and while we should be right with one another horizontally, 1 Corinthians 10:16 is not primarily a communion with each other, although it is that as well. But when we come to the Lord's Table, through faith, Christ is spiritually present with His church in a unique way. The Lord's Supper is actually a meal where Christ Himself is the host. Your lips and taste buds and stomachs actually have, in the Lord's Supper, a physical reminder of the spiritual promises of His grace. Like baptism, it is the word in visible form.

Prayer is also a means the Shepherd uses to feed His sheep. Hebrews 4:16 says, "Let us therefore come boldly to the throne of grace, that we may obtain mercy and find grace to help in time of need." Often it may seem to us that prayer is talking to an absent Lord who we hope will show up every once in a while and fill our eyes with tears, give us a particular emotion, or simply meet the request that we are bringing; but prayer is actual communication with the present Lord. Prayer is an avenue of communion with God, and it is through prayer that we are promised "grace to help in time of need."

So, let us pursue the food that the Lord gives through His particular, ordinary means of grace.

The Weekly Rhythm of the Lord's Day

It is interesting that the Lord actually gives a day, one in seven, upon which it is presumed that at least all four of these means are going to regularly happen — the Lord's Day. What do we mean by Lord's Day? In terms of the calendar, we mean Sunday. This does not mean that all days do not belong to the Lord, but simply that the Scripture calls Sunday the Lord's Day, or the day belonging to the Lord (Rev. 1:10). Christ rose on the first day of the week, and the phrase Lord's Day gets its name from the day of the Lord's resurrection, the Lord who, again, is currently present with

His church. The early church called Sunday, the first day of the week, the Lord's Day. In fact, two of Jesus' post-resurrection appearances to disciples occurred on consecutive Sundays. You can read of that in John 20:19 and 26. Two other important events in the early church happened on Sunday—Christ ascended to the right hand of the Majesty on High and He poured out His Spirit at Pentecost.

The reason we call it the Lord's Day is because that is precisely what the Bible calls it. The early church began meeting on Sunday, and public worship and rest in God began to occur on that day. Acts 20:7 says, "Now on the first day of the week, when the disciples came together to break bread, Paul, ready to depart the next day, spoke to them and continued his message until midnight." In this passage in Acts, the reference to "break bread" is likely a reference to the Lord's Table, not just to a meal. "Breaking bread" is often used as a picture for the Lord's Supper.

Elsewhere, in 1 Corinthians 16, Paul gives instructions regarding the Lord's Day as the day on which the people are to give their offerings.

> Now concerning the collection for the saints, as I have given orders to the churches of Galatia, so you must do also: 2 On the first *day* of the week let each one of you lay something aside, storing up as he may prosper, that there be no collections when I come. (1 Cor. 16:1-2)

This was a collection for the saints who were in need. Churches were partnering and associating together in the first century and their giving occurred on the Lord's Day, both in "the churches of Galatia" and in Corinth.

In the final book of the Bible, John received a vision from the Lord. In Revelation 1:10, John actually names the day for us: "I was in the Spirit on the Lord's day." This day was Sunday. Gathering weekly on the Lord's Day, Sunday, was the example of the early church. But the Christ who came to save us is not the Christ of the New Testament only. I do not think the rhythm of one and seven is something that some Jewish disciples created after Jesus' ascension. We see the rhythm of one and seven from the very beginning of the Scriptures. As far back as Genesis chapter one, we see our creating God designing all things according to a weekly rhythm. Following the creative work of days one through six, God ceased from His labor — He rested on the seventh day (Gen. 2:1-3). This pattern continues. We see it in Exodus 16, even before the codifying of the Ten Commandments in Exodus 20.

Many will argue that the Sabbath is confined to the Ten Commandments. It is there, but Sabbath is not just about the Ten Commandments. God gives the command of Sabbath as a part of His moral law. God's law in the Old Testament was one unified law about life in the land, but as a part of that law, God reveals with His own finger in stone, His moral law that transcends a mountain called Sinai. The law of God can be seen in either two groups or three groups.

Here's the two-group option: moral law and positive law. The moral law is a reflection of God's attributes revealed to us in order to establish the standard of right and wrong. It is a revelation of Himself and His nature. When He says, "Thou shalt not commit adultery," many conclude that the law of God, at this point, is a killjoy for human pleasure. But have you ever thought about the fact that God reveals something to you in that law? Specifically, God reveals that He is a God who requires that people not take other people's things. The law reveals aspects about God's nature to us, and is not just a list of prohibitions. The place where we receive God's moral law as summarily contained is the Ten Commandments, from which Jesus would later teach in the Sermon on the Mount in Matthew 5-7.

Positive law, on the other hand, is any law that God gives to a certain group of people for a certain period of time for a certain purpose, such as the Old Testament food laws, or laws of sacrifices, or for that matter, the very first command He gave in the garden to Adam and Eve regarding not eating of the tree of the knowledge of good and evil. Positive laws are indeed commands of God, but they have boundaries related to specific seasons and purposes that do not endure like the moral law does.

Another way to understand this same reality of God's law as revealed in the Old Testament is what has often been called the three-fold division of the law. This division uses the same understanding of the moral law, but also notes both the civil law (how ancient Israel was to conduct themselves as they were governed as a nation) and the ceremonial law (how they were to conduct themselves concerning the various ceremonies regarding worship as God dwelt among them, such as sacrifices, offerings, etc.). This is related to our discussion, as we shall see that the abiding moral law of God is directly related to the delightful Sabbath rhythm that God has given His people.

Interestingly, Jesus taught about the Sabbath more than many other laws. We cannot go through all of them, but very quickly, here are some common texts raised regarding Jesus and the Sabbath. Jesus says in Mark 2, "And He said to them, 'The Sabbath was made for man, and not man for the Sabbath. 'Therefore the Son of Man is also Lord of the Sabbath'" (Mark 2:27-28). The context here is that the disciples had picked grain and Jesus was getting some push back from the religious leaders. "Hey, you're picking grain. You're doing work on the Sabbath." But picking grain on the Sabbath to feed was not breaking God's law; it was ignoring the pharisaical interpretations of God's law. Jesus was a law-keeper. It is often said, however, that Jesus broke the law to prove a point that the entire Old Testament law was to be abrogated. Absolutely not! If Jesus ever broke the law, you and I are in trouble because our basis of righteousness is bound up in the active obedience of Jesus to the law of God.

His teaching in Mark 2 is interesting. Notice He does not say that the Sabbath was made for Jews. The Sabbath was made for man. Notice also He does not say that the Sabbath is abrogated. Rather, He says, in effect, "I am the Lord *of* the Sabbath" (emphasis added).

Another related passage is the Sermon on the Mount. Many will argue that there Jesus is giving a new law, having done away with the Old Testament expression of God's moral standard. However, what do we see Jesus boldly saying in Matthew 5:17? "Do not think that I came to destroy the Law or the Prophets. I did not come to destroy but to fulfill."

Another passage that is often used in this discussion to argue against an abiding Sabbath is Colossians 2:16, which says, "So let no one judge you in food or in drink, or regarding a festival or a new moon or sabbaths." Wilhemus á Brakel is most helpful in his discussion of this text. He writes:

Let us consider Colossians 2:16-17. In order to understand this text, it must first be noted that the Jews had many Sabbaths. There were *the fifteenth day* of the first month (Lev. 23:6-7), *the last day* of the Passover, and in verse 21 yet *another feast day* is mentioned. Furthermore, there are *the first day* of the seventh month (Lev. 23:24-25), the tenth day of the seventh month (Lev. 23:27-28), and the *eighth day* of the Feast of Tabernacles (vs. 36). All of these were ceremonial in nature. In addition to these there was, however, one which already had been there from the beginning, and which has been commanded in the fourth commandment of the moral law. This Sabbath was of an entirely different nature; it was of a moral nature...consider furthermore that it reads "sabbaths," and not "sabbath," since the seventh-day sabbath is generally referred to in God's Word by the singular form "sabbath"; if "sabbaths" occurs, then it occurs due to the continual repetition of every seventh day. It also needs to be considered that Paul is not speaking here to Jews who were external to the church, so that Christians would be contrasted with Jews and he was thus rebuking their religion, but to those who were within the church and by whom the weekly sabbath, also called the Lord's Day, was observed.[1]

He rightly distills the Colossian text in a way which demonstrates that the passage is not arguing against a weekly Sabbath to be observed, but that Paul is discussing particular ceremonial and festival Sabbaths which were a part of the ceremonial law of the Old Testament. This is a crucial distinction and one which many today miss in seeking to apply the passage to the idea of a weekly Sabbath.

And then there's probably the boldest related scriptural text in Hebrews 4, where we read, "There remains therefore a rest for the people of God. For he who has entered His rest has himself also ceased from his works as God did from His" (Heb. 4:9-10). I think a strong case could be made here, particularly if you read the words one by one in the original language, that the words "for He who has entered His rest" could be translated as "for the one who has entered God's rest." I think what the text is teaching is that now that Jesus has come and accomplished all that He has, and rested, and entered God's rest, our regular, practiced rest is changed in light of that. There is a Sabbath-keeping, a principle for Christians that is based on the fact that one day we will be with our Christ. So every Lord's Day is a celebration, one

---

[1] Wilhemus á Brakel, *The Christian's Reasonable Service*, vol. 3, ed. Joel R. Beeke, trans. Bartel Elshout (Grand Rapids: Reformation Heritage Books, 1994/2015), 174-76. Printed initially in 1700, I recommend the reader consider á Brakel's entire discussion on the fourth commandment for a good defense and description of the Sabbath.

day in seven, of the fact that Christ rules and reigns, and that He will take us home.

The underlying Greek word used for rest in Hebrews 4:9 (*sabbatismos*) is only and uniquely used here in the New Testament and it signifies a Sabbath practice. Various English translations pick this up. For instance, the NASB translation reads, "So then, there remains a Sabbath rest for the people of God" (Heb. 4:9). This word means a special, religiously significant period for rest and worship. So our weekly Sabbath, our weekly Lord's Day, is particularly a reminder of the resurrection rest that Christ has entered that we will also enter. It is not a doing away with of Sabbath rest as a practice. I think it is pointing us to the reality that now we have new creation rest (for the Old Testament Sabbath was tied to creation, and now, our Sabbath is tied to a creation, to a new creation).[2]

Therefore, we see the rhythm that the Lord uses as we are fed by the means of grace. Our lives are (or ought to be) driven by this weekly pattern. The Lord's Day, every Sunday, we celebrate the fact that we serve a present Lord who has been raised, and His resurrection is about our resurrection. The Lord gives us a rhythm of one in seven wherein the ordinary means of grace are particularly utilized among His people. We do not have to create patterns, for He gives us food and He gives us a rhythm—weekly Lord's Day worship. I highly encourage you to embrace this weekly rhythm. Consider that God has given it to you as a gift, not as a burden. Embrace it by a dutiful attention to the ordinary means of grace, of ceasing from the

---

[2] I encourage the reader to consult the following resources. Richard C. Barcellos, *Getting the Garden Right: Adam's Work and God's Rest in Light of Christ* (Cape Coral, FL: Founders Press, 2017) for a fuller treatment of these issues, including a chapter on Heb. 4. A lengthy resource on understanding the law of God would be Philip E. Ross, *From the Finger of God: The Biblical and Theological Basis for the Threefold Division of the Law* (Ross-shire, Scotland: Christian Focus, Mentor Imprint, 2010).

labors and recreations of the other six days, and give attention, all the day long, to the rest into which Christ is taking His people. The Sabbath is a biblical rhythm the Lord has given and He is so faithful to have done so.

The Fence the Lord Provides

Not only does our shepherd feed us, and feed us in a weekly rhythm through the ordinary means of grace, but He also provides a fence or a sheep pen for us. This pen is the local church, a body with which we are intimately connected, one that we should not abandon. Hebrews 10:25 says that we should not forsake the assembling together of the body of believers. In other words, we shouldn't keep ourselves from assembling weekly with the body of Christ. Here again, if Christ is present and the means of grace are the things that He is using in a weekly rhythm for us, isn't God good to tell us not to forsake such a rich banquet? When I used to hear about individuals not gathering on the Lord's Day, I would think, "Oh, that is not good. It's sinful." Now I am saddened and I think about how they are missing access to the ordinary means of grace. They are trying to go it alone. The Lord has given a rhythm and a food and a fence in the church assembled locally, and these straying sheep are grazing in the weeds.

Fences protect. The church is a sheep pen; a structure or a boundary around God's people, and while the church is a universal reality, the Scriptures give no picture of the church not locally gathered. The church is regularly, locally assembled, and that is the fence, or structure, that the Lord uses. He feeds us in a rhythm, a regular rhythm, and He puts a local fence around us to help us to see that He is leading, caring for, and protecting His people. Ephesians gives us the picture of Christ ruling over His church as the gathered people of God. The local church is a specific, tangible fence around which the Lord feeds His sheep in a weekly pattern.

Our opening bookend was Ephesians in seeing the Lord as presently ruling over His church, feeding His sheep in a regular rhythm that He has given. We do not have to wonder where the next meal is coming from with our Shepherd in charge. And lastly we have seen that He gives us a fence to protect us which is the church gathered.

Conclusion

Let me give a closing bookend for this whole book. We stated at the beginning that all of this is predicated, or based, upon the idea that Christ is a present Shepherd who leads His church in green pastures. Let us close with the bookend of one of the last passages of Scripture, Revelation 1. John saw a vision on the Lord's Day, Sunday, and let's catch a glimpse of this. Notice two things: seven churches and Christ among them.

> Then I turned to see the voice that spoke with me. And having turned I saw seven golden lampstands, [13] and in the midst of the seven lampstands *One* like the Son of Man, clothed with a garment down to the feet and girded about the chest with a golden band. [14] His head and hair *were* white like wool, as white as snow, and His eyes like a flame of fire; [15] His feet *were* like fine brass, as if refined in a furnace, and His voice as the sound of many waters (Rev. 1:12-15)

Do not lose that image, Christian. I do not think that this is just for those seven churches. In this passage, contextually they are primary, but do not lose the reality of the Lord Christ walking among His churches, His fenced-in ones that He is protecting with a weekly supply of food. This self-same Christ walks among His churches today. He is present and we are getting a glimpse of this through this passage. Notice, in the midst of Christ standing among His churches, His voice is heard. The passage continues:

> He had in His right hand seven stars, out of His mouth went a sharp two-edged sword, and His countenance *was* like the sun shining in its strength. [17] And when I saw Him, I fell at His feet as dead. But He laid His right hand on me, saying to me, "Do not be afraid; I am the First and the Last. [18] "I *am* He who lives, and was dead, and behold, I am alive forevermore. Amen. And I have the keys of Hades and of Death." (Rev. 1:16-18)

Christ is present with His church and He uniquely makes Himself known in the food that He gives through the means of grace. This Christ described here is Head over His church and He is currently present with it through the Spirit.

What do we see, then, as we end our look into the means of grace? We see that our Shepherd is present and He gives us food—regular, spiritual nourishment through the ordinary means of grace. Our present Lord also gives us a rhythm, the Lord's Day. It doesn't mean that He will not come to you at midnight on a Friday night when you're in distress. It doesn't mean that He's not present over the church Thursday morning at a Bible study. But He gives us a consistent, ordered rhythm so that we might know a weekly central time wherein He will meet with and feed His sheep. That is His plan. And lastly, we see a fence: a gathered people, as Christ is among them. Jesus uses the picture of sheep and a shepherd when He describes the church and the care He takes for His people.

As parents of four children, my wife and I have found the importance of family mealtime. These meals are not just time for fellowship and sharing, but also the regular nourishing rhythm of providing food for our children. They need the food offered in these regular meals to grow and be fed. However, sometimes one or more of our little ones will avoid parts of the meal, or not eat what is on their plate. Later, however, once mealtime is finished, there is a desire for a snack because they had not gotten the food they needed. How often we capitulated in those early years and allowed the snack closet to be utilized. Then we wondered why at mealtime they were not hungry. Once we saw the pattern, we realized how important it was to stress the nutrition of our regular meals, eaten in a rhythm as a family. They needed the nutrients of the food, not the fluff of the snacks. Similarly, we need the spiritual nourishment of the ordinary means of grace and yet, so often, we allow ourselves, and our churches, to focus on "snacks" when the rhythm of true spiritual food is really what we need. The ordinary means of grace are the regular meals the Lord Christ has given to us so that we do not have to resort to lesser snacks. That is what our present Christ has done for His church. You don't have to go it alone or find meal replacements. In fact, if you do, you will be malnourished.

At the beginning of our church worship services on the Lord's Day, I will sometimes remind the body of believers that, in our worship, we are gathering at the outskirts of heaven. Every Lord's Day when we gather, when we are around the Table, or when we hear the word preached, or when we pray, we are right on the outskirts of the praises of heaven. What greater earthly gift could we have? In a day when many want to hunt for the next spiritual tool, seminar, book, device, or gimmick, we need to understand that while the Lord uses a myriad of things in the life of every believer, He has promised that by the ordinary means of grace— preaching, baptism, the Lord's Supper, and prayer—He will bless and grow His people in grace. These are the lush green feeding grounds to which we must turn often. We are blessed, indeed, as we are fed in the green pastures of our Lord.

A Psalm of David.

The Lord *is* my shepherd; I shall not want.

He makes me to lie down in green pastures; He leads me beside the still waters.

He restores my soul; He leads me in the paths of righteousness For His name's sake.

Yea, though I walk through the valley of the shadow of death, I will fear no evil; For You *are* with me; Your rod and Your staff, they comfort me.

You prepare a table before me in the presence of my enemies; You anoint my head with oil; My cup runs over.

Surely goodness and mercy shall follow me All the days of my life; And I will dwell in the house of the Lord Forever.

(Psalm 23)

Study Questions

1. How is the Lord's Day connected to the means of grace?

2. In what ways do the Scriptures demonstrate that the Sabbath continues for God's people?

3. Why is the local church particularly necessary and important for the Christian over and above other types of ministries?

4. What benefits does the rhythm of one day in seven provide for the Christian?